THE PRESENCE OF
THE KINGDOM

THE PRESENCE OF
THE KINGDOM

JACQUES ELLUL

Introduction by
WILLIAM STRINGFELLOW

A CROSSROAD BOOK
THE SEABURY PRESS • NEW YORK

TRANSLATED BY OLIVE WYON

First *Seabury Paperback* Edition Published 1967
Fifth Printing

Copyright by Editions Roulet, 1948
All rights reserved
Library of Congress Catalog Card Number: 67-21833
574-273-C-9-4-5

PRINTED IN THE UNITED STATES OF AMERICA

CONTENTS

INTRODUCTION

DURING the last few years in the English-speaking world, there has been published in translation three massive, important, scholarly studies of contemporary society by Jacques Ellul—*The Technological Society, Propaganda,* and *Political Illusions.* Any one of these studies in itself would, under ordinary circumstances, be considered a notable achievement; the three together make for an incisive probing of our contemporary world. Because of the achievement which they constitute, Jacques Ellul's earlier slight volume, *The Presence of the Kingdom (Présence au Monde Moderne),* might easily be overlooked, yet in that book Ellul laid down the perspective from which his subsequent penetrating criticism of society would be made. In a real sense, *The Presence of the Kingdom* is Jacques Ellul's most astonishing book.

In both Europe and the United States, many—and I include myself—regard *The Presence of the Kingdom* as an authentically prophetic work. Even those who assess it more modestly cannot fail to find it breathtakingly far-sighted. First published in France a generation ago, the book evidences an uncanny and virtually unerring perception of the forces and issues of contemporary social change which plague men and nations—and which,

1

therefore, beset Christians in the world. Ellul not only anticipates the imminence of sophisticated technics, the dehumanizing tyrannies of mass media, and the perils of thermonuclear diplomacy, but also apprehends the relentless conflicts of ideologies among themselves and men, and then foresees a triumph of the totalitarian spirit, which has by now been substantially institutionalized in the United States and in Ellul's own country.

The thought of Jacques Ellul became known in both theological and legal quarters in America through the publication of *The Presence of the Kingdom* and, notably, *The Theological Foundation of Law*. These two works were widely used a decade ago in preparation for a national conference on theology and law and have achieved a controversial impact upon the dialogue in this country concerning theological ethics.

One reason that Ellul's thinking has been provocative, especially in the United States, is that his theological insights are authenticated by diligence in biblical study and by the intense involvement of the man in the very social crises that he seeks to address theologically. Jacques Ellul is no pedantic theologian discussing ideas like a dilettante whose convictions are never baptized in action. On the contrary, in Ellul one finds that ideas and acts are so integral one to the other that his decisions and actions in actual life are an incarnation of what he thinks and writes. His witness as a Christian has been nurtured in danger and turbulence, not in sanctuary or detachment. He was a militant in the French resistance to the Nazis; he has served in politics as Deputy Mayor of Bordeaux; he is distinguished professionally in the law and in economics; he was among the remnant who were concerned to expose and oppose the atrocities of the French military in the Algerian war; he is esteemed in ecumenical councils as a creative theologian; he is a partisan of renewal and relevance in the Reformed Church of France; he became a Christian in consequence of his immersion in the saga of the Bible while engaged in the strife of the world. In short, he is one who speaks with authority. This being so, it is not surprising that his words provoke controversy within the churches and in society.

There is another reason, however, for the influence of Ellul's thinking in America. His theological ethics illuminate two peculiar omissions in a realm long overlooked by theologians and preachers in the United States, omissions which have caused the social witness of American Christians to be inane and sometimes inarticulate. These omissions concern matters so related that they may be regarded as two dimensions of the same concept.

The first is the failure to identify the power of death as the ruler of this world. Christians in America seldom consider this at all, supposing that such talk is of medieval vintage, having no reference to the realities of the present day. Or they regard the identification as a quaint myth, part of a fairy-tale schema of the faith appropriate —if at all—for Sunday-school children. Or they make use of the identification as a kind of Easter Sunday rhetoric to adorn the seasonal sermon on spring, or else they exploit it as something to be taken to heart as a sanction for personal fundamentalistic pietism. But few books by American authors purporting to deal with theological ethics discern the presence and power of death in this world, in this day, even in America, as an essential clue, to nations and institutions as well as to individuals, of their radical alienation from one another and from themselves, that is to say, of their fallenness.

Ellul's theology troubles Americans because the lucidity of his theological ethics on this point discloses the naïveté of theirs. He does not flinch from naming Satan as the apparent ruler of this world, yet he does not manipulate language when he speaks in this way; instead, he clothes it with meaning which is unambiguous and as contemporaneous as one can be. Thus, for Ellul, to write of Satan militant in this world means, for instance, the will to death, the affirmation of death as ultimate reality and—hence—the ground for immediate moral decision, an idolatry of death in which all men and all societies are caught up. Medieval? It is as timely as the casualty reports from Vietnam. Myth? In what other term than suicide can the American racial crisis be empirically described? Rhetoric? Listen to the demands for uncritical obedience to the graven image of the nation's manifest destiny and therein hear the voices of the acolytes of death. A mere sanction for narrow pietism? Behold the individual who seeks to accomplish his own salvation, and ultimately discerns, for all his futile effort, only death. Had Jacques Ellul been an American, he could not have addressed Americans more cogently and pastorally than he does in this book; nor could he have sensed more sharply the present confusion that afflicts and enfeebles the Christian witness in American society.

The coincident omission in the sphere of theological ethics in America to which Ellul brings enlightenment is the failure to comprehend the work of the Holy Spirit. Christians in the United States, or at least churchy folk here, have a notorious reputation ecumenically for sentimental verbosity about the Holy Spirit. It is mainly a rather nebulous abstraction profanely evoked, or, what is just as vulgar, a visceral phenomenon that is blamed on the Holy Spirit. Sitting in a pew, not a few laymen of the American churches notice that the name of the Holy Spirit is usually mentioned when the clergy seem otherwise at a loss for words. The name is commonly mentioned without regard for liturgical integrity—which is profoundly offensive to anyone who affirms liturgy (as the Jews of the Old Testament did) as an application and enactment of theological ethics. Sitting at a desk or standing at a workbench or otherwise employed or engaged in the world, laymen are not likely to see that the work of the Holy Spirit refers to anything practical, decisional, or empirical. In fact, it literally has reference for them to *nothing* in their experience.

Meanwhile those in America who have chosen theological ethics as a discipline have, for the most part, ignored both the Holy Spirit and the work of the Holy Spirit as central to any scheme of Christian ethics, particularly social, as distinguished from individualistic, ethics. Not so with Jacques Ellul. He writes, in this book, of the historicity of the Holy Spirit in terms at once biblically responsible and actually recognizable. He discerns that the presence and vitality of the Holy Spirit in this time has to do with the imprint and shape and scope of the Word of God upon all history and with the perpetual, redundant, resilient truth of the Word of God throughout all of history. After all, there is some content in the Word of God, in the biblical witness, but no less in the rest of history whether before or since the Bible. This content is substantive, definite and identifiable, and, in the peculiar inheritance of Christians, is named the Holy Spirit. In the theology of Ellul the recurrent and cosmic drama of the will to death is transcended, through the work of the Holy Spirit, by the will to life, bringing freedom from idolatry of death—in the forms of nationalism, racism, ideology, personal lusts, class distinction, professionalism, or human philosophy. For Ellul, since death is real and the power of death is thus proved great, if not almighty, so is the Holy Spirit actualized in the everyday and immediate issues of existence by the emancipation from the power of death signaled in the Resurrection—and dispensed so extravagantly thereby.

To put it all more succinctly, and in other words, Americans live, both in their society and in the churches of this society, so insulated from the gospel, therefore so distorted in the region of ethics—and in that most esoteric precinct called theological ethics—that we had better listen to the extraordinary witness that is Jacques Ellul.

WILLIAM STRINGFELLOW

Easter Monday, 1967
New York City

I

THE CHRISTIAN IN
THE WORLD

AT the very outset of these studies it seems necessary
to re-emphasize certain familiar Biblical truths;
such reminders are never irrelevant; to-day they are
more necessary than ever.

I

The Bible tells us that the Christian is in the world,
and that there he must remain. The Christian has
not been created in order to separate himself from, or
to live aloof from the world. When this separation is
effected, it will be God's doing, not man's; this final
separation will take place at the end of time, when God
will 'gather the wheat into His barn,' but the tares
will be rooted up and burned. Similarly, Christians
are not meant to live together in closed groups, refusing
to mix with other people. The Christian community
must never be a closed body. Thus if the Christian is
necessarily *in* the world, he is not *of* it. This means
that his thought, his life, and his heart are not controlled
by the world, and do not depend upon the world, for
they belong to another Master. Thus, since he belongs
to another Master, the Christian has been sent into

this world by this Master, and his communion with his Master remains unbroken, in spite of the 'world' in which he has to live.

But this communion of the Christian with Jesus Christ has some serious implications: first of all, the Christian, by this very fact, finds that he is not confronted by the material forces of the world but by its spiritual reality. Because he is in communion with Jesus Christ he has to fight not against flesh and blood but against 'the principalities, against the powers, against the world-rulers of this darkness.' At the same time this communion assures him that he does not belong to the world, that he is free from the fatality of the world which is moving towards death, and, as a result of this liberation by grace, he *can* fight against the spiritual realities of the world. To speak quite plainly, he is called to break the fatality which hangs over the world, and he *can* do so. In order to do this, by the grace of God he receives the necessary weapons.[1]

If this, then, is the Christian's situation, what part should he play in the life of the world? It is only too easy to reply: to 'witness,' to 'evangelize,' or 'to lead a Christian life,' or again 'to act according to the will of God.' All this is true, of course, but so long as it is not really understood, so long as each answer is only a traditional formula, it leads us nowhere. Now it is the Bible which shows us what the Christian 'calling' really is; it enables us to understand this situation, and it shows us what concrete action is required.

First of all, we need to remember that the Christian must not act in exactly the same way as everyone else. He has a part to play in this world which no one else can possibly fulfil. He is not asked to look at the various

[1] Eph. 6.10–20.

movements which men have started, choose those which seem 'good,' and then support them. He is not asked to give his blessing to any particular human enterprise, nor to support the decisions of man. He is charged with a mission of which the natural man can have no idea; yet in reality this mission is decisive for the actions of men. For it is on this that the truth or error of human action depends.

If the Christian works with all his might at some human project he is only a human being like others, and his effort is worth no more than that; but if he accepts his specific function as a Christian (which does not necessarily entail his material or effective participation in the world), this is decisive for human history.

God has not sent him into the world for any other purpose than to fulfil this function. But this specific function cannot be compared with other human ends; it cannot be understood by the 'natural man'; yet the significance of all other functions depends upon it. This function is defined by the Scriptures in three ways:[1]

1. You are the salt of the earth.
2. You are the light of the world.
3. I send you forth as sheep in the midst of wolves.

To be the salt of the earth is a precise reference to Leviticus 2.13, where we are told that salt is the sign of the covenant between God and Israel. Thus, in the sight of men and in the reality of this world, the Christian is a visible sign of the new covenant which God has made with this world in Jesus Christ. But it is essential that the Christian should really *be* this sign, that is to say, that in his life and his words he should allow this covenant to be manifest in the eyes of men. Apart from that, this earth will feel bereft of any

[1] Cf. *Wending* nr. 11; p. 625.

'covenant'; it will not know where it is going; it will no longer have any real knowledge of itself, nor any certainty about its preservation. The fact that Christians *are*, in their lives, the 'salt of the earth,' does far more for the preservation of the world than any external action.

To be the light of the world: 'And the light shineth in the darkness and the darkness apprehendeth it not.'[1] Christians *are* this light, through Christ; this may be understood in a twofold sense:

First of all, the light eliminates the darkness; it is that which separates life from death; it is that which gives us the criterion of goodness (that is why in the text[2] this phrase is immediately followed by a reference to 'good works'). Strictly speaking, apart from this light we cannot know what a 'good work' is, nor in what 'goodness' consists.

From another point of view this 'light of the world' is that which gives meaning and direction to the history of the world, and thus explains it. In the succession of events which the course of history presents, there is no logic, no certitude, but this logic is supplied by the presence of the Church, however strange this may seem. This is why, by being the 'light,' the Christian is an element in the life of the world; now, however, in addition to the work of 'preservation,' he goes further: he reveals to the world the truth about its condition, and witnesses to the salvation of which he is an instrument.

Like sheep in the midst of wolves: here again the Christian is a 'sign' of the reality of God's action. It is the Lamb of God, Jesus Christ, who takes away the sins

[1] John 1.5 (R.V.).
[2] Matt. 5.14–16.

of the world. But every Christian is treated like his Master, and every Christian receives from Jesus Christ a share in His work. He is a 'sheep' not because his action or his sacrifice has a purifying effect on the world, but because he is the living and real 'sign,' constantly renewed in the midst of the world, of the sacrifice of the Lamb of God. In the world everyone wants to be a 'wolf,' and no one is called to play the part of a 'sheep.' Yet the world cannot *live* without this living witness of sacrifice. That is why it is essential that Christians should be very careful not to be 'wolves' in the spiritual sense—that is, people who try to dominate others. Christians must accept the domination of other people, and offer the daily sacrifice of their lives, which is united with the sacrifice of Jesus Christ.

These biblical phrases ought not to be understood as mere metaphors, as terms which we use when we are speaking of Christians. This language is not just a 'way of speaking,' a pleasant picture. We are only too much inclined to understand such phrases as figures of speech or as poetry. Nor is this quality of living something which 'happens' to the Christian accidentally. People often say too easily that the Christian possesses this quality, but that he could have other qualities.

On the contrary, all these expressions denote a stark reality, from which it is impossible to escape. Here Jesus Christ confronts us with the specific function of the Christian—and there can be no other. Things cannot be otherwise; the Christian has no choice, and if he does not accept this function, he does not fulfil the part assigned to him. He then betrays both Jesus Christ and the world. Of course he can always immerse himself in good works, and pour out his energy in religious or social activities, but all this will

have no meaning unless he is fulfilling the only mission
with which he has been charged by Jesus Christ, which
is first of all *to be a sign*.

This situation is that of all Christians, but it becomes
acute for the layman, because he, in particular, cannot
be separated from the world. He cannot have any
illusions on this subject. Primarily he is involved in
the life of the world through his work and his interests.
He is constantly attacked in his own person by this
'world.' It becomes more and more difficult for him to
imagine that a Christian can live apart from 'the
world.' More than ever, every person is involved in the
life of the world, and the world is more penetrating,
more crushing, more exacting, than it has ever been.
One's profession itself is sufficient to-day to absorb all
the vital forces of man. Each of us is immersed in this
overflowing activity, which leaves us no time to reflect,
nor to fulfil our function as Christians, nor even to live.
And just as the Christian is not free to lead his life
as he would like to do, so also the Christian layman has
to submit to a mechanical solidarity which hinders him
from playing the drama of the faith. He is part of the
whole body of men, whether he wishes it or not, and
this is much more true, materially speaking, in the
world of the present day than it would have been in
earlier civilizations. It is now impossible to be isolated,
to be separate. The illusion of a Christian life attached
to a convent or a hermitage has vanished. Whether it
be due to the simple material fact of communications,
or to the interdependence of economic institutions, or
to the growth of democracy, in every way these influences combine to force man into this solidarity with

others. Thus the Christian cannot consider himself pure, as compared with others. He cannot declare that he is free from the sin of the world. A major fact of our present civilization is that more and more sin becomes collective, and the individual is forced to participate in collective sin. Everyone bears the consequences of the faults of others. This becomes particularly poignant when nations are at war, for instance, but it is true of all social situations. It is still an illusion of a Christian life which is disappearing that it is possible to be 'perfect' in the midst of a lost world.

Modern man can no longer have confidence in the virtues of the individual, in his kindness, or his energy, because we are no longer confronted by individual sins but by the state of sin of humanity. This ancient truth of the Bible is now visible to all. Our society is a manifestation, which cannot be challenged, of the revelation of God on the subject of our sin: 'There is none righteous, no, not one.'[1] And this is not because, regarded as individuals, all men are bad, but because all are 'shut up under sin,'[2] because there is a solidarity of all men in sin, and this solidarity is not only spatial, but historical; this makes us one with those who have died in their sins, right back to original sin itself. The world of the present day teaches us that this doctrine is neither an idea nor an explanation. It is a statement of a reality, which is just as concrete as the solidarity of all men in modern war.

This situation is, however, disagreeable for a Christian. The priest or the pastor will feel it less, the layman cannot escape it. But he will do all he possibly can to escape it, and we see such attempts taking place

[1] Romans 3.10.
[2] Gal. 3.22.

in two directions. Some will try to dissociate the spiritual situation from the material one, despising the material situation, denying that it has any meaning, declaring that it is neutral, and does not concern eternal life, and that we can turn our attention solely to 'spiritual problems.' Such people argue that nothing matters but 'the interior life': that is, that to be the 'salt' or the 'light' is a purely spiritual affirmation, which has no practical consequences. This is exactly what Jesus Christ calls hypocrisy. It means giving up any attempt to live out one's religion in the world. It turns the living person of Jesus Christ into an abstraction. God became incarnate—it is not for us to undo His work. This dissociation of our life into two spheres: the one 'spiritual,' where we can be 'perfect,' and the other material and unimportant: where we behave like other people, is one of the reasons why the Churches have so little influence on the world. This avoidance of responsibility for our faith is evidently a convenient solution of the intolerable dilemma in which we are placed by the society of our day. All we can say is: that this is the exact opposite of what Jesus Christ wills for us, and of that which He came to do.

Another solution, which is more frequently attempted, consists in the desire to 'moralize' or 'christianize' the actions of the world. If the State were Christian, how agreeable it would be to depend upon it; then let us make a Christian State, etc. People who take this line aim at having a kind of 'Christian conception' of things: they want to have 'good' institutions, 'good' morals; they want to know what is 'the good' in every situation, and thus to gloss over the actual situation of our present world, covering it up with an ethical 'glaze'—'Colour-wash the devil in gold, dress him up in white, and perhaps he will become an angel'! It is this effort to paint a different picture, which all Christian ethics or sociologies or politics, or even social Christianity, offer us as a solution. People try to bring a Christian colouring into the acts and situations of the world, either by explaining and justifying them by a good theology, or by giving them a blessing, or by trying to 'apply' Christian remedies and Christian virtues to them. To sum up, in all these hypotheses people are trying to make tolerable the situation in which the world puts us. Just as they try to show that it is possible to be a soldier, or a banker—and a Christian, so also social disorder and human misery are justified by doing 'good works.' What people are really trying to do in all these movements, is to see to it that the condition of the world is not *too* shocking for the Christian conscience. In reality men are trying to make a bridge between the world and the Kingdom of God, and the Christian would find himself always upon the bridge! The bridge would be ethics, with its accompaniment of good works, and a good conscience.

But this effort to put an end both to the scandal that the world ought to be for faith, and that faith ought to be for the world, is in reality the most anti-Christian position any one could possibly adopt. In the studies which follow, we shall be concerned with the effort to see, when confronted by some of the profound problems which the world provides for us, how the Christian is implicated, what is his situation, and particularly that there is no possible solution in the sense of 'appeasement' and satisfaction.

From what point of view, then, should the question be asked? Here I have no intention of trying to say anything new. All I want to do is to re-discover what has always been a perfectly familiar Christian truth, but one that Christians always try to forget, because it is very upsetting, and even intolerable. The first element in this situation is this: we must not weaken the opposition that exists between the Christian faith, the claims of revelation, and life in the world and its demands, its faults, and its compromises.

The fact of living in the world, from which we ought not to escape, is a stumbling-block for our faith. It ought to be so, and so it must remain. We have no right to accustom ourselves to this world, nor to try to hide it from ourselves with Christian illusions. Living in the world we are living in the domain of the Prince of this world, of Satan, and all around us we constantly see the action of this Prince, and the result of the state of sin in which we are all placed without exception, because in spite of all our efforts and our piety we share in the sin of the world. We are involved in it because in spite of our faith we are and remain sinners; we are also involved in the sin of humanity through the various 'orders' of life created by God, so that when a man of my family, or of my nation, commits a sin, I am responsible before God for this transgression. Only this truth must not remain a merely verbal one.

What does it mean to share in the life of the world like this? First of all, we must consider not only our sins as individuals, but also our sin which is due to the fact that we are men and women living in the world, and belonging to the world. Henceforth we must give up the idea that we can decrease our sin by our virtues.

We must give up believing that we can 'improve' the world, that at least we can make man better, even if we cannot make him happy. At the same time, if we take this situation of the Christian seriously, we must refuse to further the disintegrating tendency in the world. We must not say to ourselves, 'We can't do anything about it!' To talk like this is to play into the hands of the Prince of this world. Thus we seem caught between two necessities, which nothing can alter: on the one hand it is impossible for us to make this world less sinful; on the other hand it is impossible for us to accept it as it is. If we refuse either the one or the other, we are actually not accepting the situation in which God has placed us. He has sent us into the world, and just as we are involved in the tension of sin and of grace, so also we are involved in the tension between these two contradictory demands. It is a very painful, and a very uncomfortable, situation, but it is the only position which can be fruitful for the action of the Christian in the world, and for his life in the world. First of all, we must accept this tension, and live in it. We must accept—in a spirit of repentance—the fact that our life in this world is necessarily 'scandalous,' knowing that it cannot be otherwise, and that to imagine that it could be otherwise is hypocrisy. But to know our true situation in the world implies that we really know the problems of the world. To be honest, we must not accept this tension of the Christian, or of the Christian life, as an abstract truth. It must be *lived*, it must be realized, in the most concrete and living way possible. On the other hand, Christians ought to realize that to achieve this is the only real way of helping the world, from the social, economic, and political point of view.

It is characteristic of the world in these spheres that it poses false problems. Of himself the natural man is incapable of seeing the spiritual reality in which he is struggling. He only sees the surface of social, political, and economic problems, and he tries to work on this surface with technical methods, and in accordance with moral standards. In this way, man only gets more and more deeply involved in false and complicated situations, until the collapse of all that he calls his 'civilization.'

What part should the Christian play in these questions? First of all, it is not for him to define the problems in the same terms as those who have no faith; it is not for him to tinker with futile attempts at technical and moral 'solutions'; his job is to discover the real spiritual difficulties which every political or economic situation contains. So far as the solution is concerned, it cannot be a rational one: it can only be a solution in terms of *life*, and the acceptance of forgiveness given in Jesus Christ.[1] In other words, it is in receiving, and in living the Gospel that political, economic, and other questions can be solved. Thus it is the acceptance of this tension (already mentioned) which alone permits us to discover the true social situation; it alone helps us to respond to it by a human attitude which is not a lie, nor an illusion.

On the other hand, the fact that the layman accepts this tension in his life, and lives it out to the full, is the human condition required if theology is to re-discover a message for the world. It is the actual price which must be paid, if any point of contact is to be created between the language of the Christian faith and that of

[1] Cf. the articles on social and political problems by J. Ellul in *Foi et Vie* (1947–1948).

the modern pagan. In reality, to-day the theologian has nothing to say to the world, because there are no 'laymen' in our churches; because, on the one hand, there is the minister, who does not know the situation in the world, and on the other hand, there are 'laymen,' who are very careful to keep their faith and their life in different compartments, or who try to escape from this dilemma by concentrating on ethics. Theological truth has no point of contact with the world. This does not mean that we doubt whether the Holy Spirit (and He alone) can establish this contact; but it means that we have to recognize that throughout the course of history God uses material means—-in other words, He acts by His Spirit through human instruments. Now it is this human instrument that our churches lack; that is why, when the Gospel is preached, its message no longer reaches the world. The channel through which the Gospel should reach the world—and does not— ought to be the 'layman,' living the tension which we have just described. He is the 'point of contact' between the ideologies of the world in which he lives and theology—between economic realities, and the forgiveness of Jesus Christ for those realities, which cannot otherwise be altered in the sight of God. Indeed, we might almost say that the experience of the Christian layman is the theologian's material for his knowledge of humanity.

On the other hand, the layman is more than a guinea-pig! When he 'lives' this tension every day of his life, the fact of his presence leads the Church to recognize the value and the truth of the anguish of the world; while the world learns to recognize its real problems, behind the lies which it tries to perpetuate in order to avoid listening to the Word of God. Thus the position of the layman's life is essential, both to the Church and to the world. Consequently it is essential that this position should be clearly seen and understood.

But this does not exhaust the problem of the reality of the situation of the Christian in the world. He must try to live in such a way in his daily life that his actions are in accordance with the ideas we have been discussing, e.g. as 'the salt of the earth,' 'the light of the world,' and 'as sheep in the midst of wolves.' But these truths should not be regarded merely as 'Christian principles,' but should take concrete form, and become a vital element in daily life.

In reality, the problem that confronts us is that of the Christian ethic, an ethic which has nothing in common with what is generally called 'morality,' and still less with the Christian 'virtues' in the traditional sense. It is evident that neither a theological decision, nor an intellectual argument, even if it be based upon the Christian revelation, will enable us to know the Christian ethic. At heart, this is a fight of faith: individual, and in the presence of God; and a living attitude, adopted according to the measure of faith of each person, and as the result of his or her faith. It is never a series of rules, or principles, or slogans, and every Christian is really responsible for his works and for his conscience. Thus we can never make a complete and valid description of the ethical demands of God, any more than we can reach its heart. We can only define its outline, and its conditions, and study some of its elements for purposes of illustration.

The heart of this ethic may be expressed thus: it is based upon an 'agonistic' way of life; that is to say, the

Christian life is always an 'agony,'[1] that is, a final, decisive conflict; thus it means that constant and actual presence in our hearts of the two elements of judgment and of grace. But it is this very fact which ensures our liberty. We are free, because at every moment in our lives we are both judged and pardoned, and are consequently placed in a new situation, free from fatalism, and from the bondage of sinful habits. To go further is the affair of the theologian, but this is enough to show us that the whole Christian attitude is in direct relation with the act of God in Jesus Christ.

The two dominant characters of this ethic are, so it seems to me: (a) that it should be temporary; and (b) that it should be apologetic.

(a) *Temporary:* because it concerns a given and variable situation. We are not concerned with formulating principles, but with knowing how to judge an action in given circumstances. Thus we are not bound to hold closely to moral ideas which must be invariable, but the Scripture teaches us that its ethic varies in form, and in concrete application to situations and places. This may sound surprising, after what I have just said about the heart of ethics. People might say: 'Then there is no system at all, there are no given data, and that the whole of the Christian ethic consists simply in letting every Christian act according to his faith.' In reality it is nothing of the kind. There are consequences of faith which can be objectively indicated. To say the contrary suggests that we are all angels, that we are all already in the Kingdom of God, and that our flesh no longer offers any resistance to the action of the Spirit. At present we are still in this 'body of death.' The construction of a Christian ethic is

---

[1] Gk. ἀγωνία: a contest, wrestling.

necessary, first of all, because it is a guide, an indication given to faith, a real assistance to the brethren; and then, because it allows us to give a real concrete content to the judgment which God pronounces upon us; and, finally, because it is necessary for the life of the Church. But this elaboration must not be substituted for the fight of faith, which every Christian must wage; that is why it is indicative, not imperative. We must not imagine that this ethic will give us the permanent solution of all problems. That is why, essentially, it ought to be temporary; it needs to be continually revised, re-examined, and re-shaped by the combined effort of the Church as a whole.

(*b*) Further, the Christian ethic is necessarily *apologetic* in character. This statement, however, should not be taken in the usual sense of the defence and demonstration of Christian truth, that is to say, as an intellectual operation. This 'apology' (which cannot really be accomplished by man) is that which is mentioned in Matthew 5.16: 'Even so let your light shine before men, that they may see your good works, and glorify your Father which is in Heaven.' That is to say, that the 'works' done in virtue of, and in consequence of, the Christian ethic, ought to appear in the light of Jesus Christ as veritable good works. Of itself the world is incapable of seeing these good works. It can only do so in this light, and we must see to it that our works proceed so directly from the action of Jesus Christ in us, that the world will see them in their true light. This implies that we do not need to refer to the judgment of the world in order to estimate the value of our 'good works,' but that, on the contrary, we have to constrain the world to see them as they are; we, on our part, must see to it that these 'works' are of such a quality that they lead men to praise God. When they do this, they do constitute an apologetic. Our ethic as a whole will have no meaning unless it is directed towards this conflict with the world which should end in giving glory to God. The ethic created by the Church should be the result of this tension in which every Christian is involved. It is the reflection of this conflict, and the whole aim of this ethic is to direct this conflict towards the glory of God.

Thus we see that the Christian ethic is inseparable from the preaching of the Word, for the very behaviour of the Christian destroys the work of Satan, and helps to build up the Body of Christ in the world. Finally, we must come back to this idea that the Christian ethic is not a means of resolving the Christian tension—that it is not a recipe for righteousness; that it is not a synthesis of the Christian faith and the world's values; that it is not a way of enabling the Christian to live without the Holy Spirit. It is the very opposite of all this.

This problem of ethics does not cover the whole situation of the Christian in the world; it is only a description of his action. Now this action is only one element in the whole situation, placed between the actual situation (that is, the tension which must be accepted), and the Christian's participation in the preservation of the world, which is a result of the application of the Christian ethic.

The Christian must participate in the preservation of the world; he must work effectively for it. But there are some serious misunderstandings on this point which we must try to dissipate. When we speak of the preservation of the world, immediately we envisage participation in the actions which the world thinks are best for it.

The world chooses its own methods, draws up its own plan of action in order to solve its problems; and people often think that if Christians are to help to preserve the world they ought to join in these movements.

Thus when everyone was shocked by the demonic character of the Nazi *régime*, war was presented as a crusade. The world took up arms; Christians took up the same arms, and fought in exactly the same way as others against these demonic forces. Similarly, in the problem of reconstruction, many Christians, and many of the best, preached the same methods of reconstruction, and urged other men to follow the path chosen by the world; for instance, they would say that 'the United Nations is an admirable institution and full of hope for the future'; or that 'above all we must produce material goods,' and that 'the prefabricated house is the solution of all our problems.' I have even read in an extremely Christian (Catholic) review that 'the washing-machine would help to save France.'

I believe that at this point there is a serious confusion of thought. It is not in doing exactly the same as other people, and in carrying out technical work, that the Christian 'participates effectively' in the 'preservation of the world,' but in fulfilling his specific rôle, which we have just described. | This does not mean that technical work ought not to be done, or that it is useless, but this work is done by everybody, and it has no meaning unless it is guided, accompanied, and sustained by another work that only the Christian can do, and that he often does *not* do. For the world ought to be preserved by God's methods, not by man's technical work (which can, however, be used by God and form part of His activity, on condition that men bring the whole sphere of technics under His judgment and His control). Further, the world ought to be preserved in a certain *order*, willed by God, and not according to the plan that men make of this order (a plan, however, which *may* be accepted by God on condition that men are genuinely concerned for truth and justice). Thus, when we were confronted by Hitler—if it be true that he represented a satanic power—first of all there was a spiritual conflict to be waged. It is prayer which should be decisive, but we no longer have any confidence in the extraordinary power of prayer. Prayer is the power which exorcises demons, by the Holy Spirit, and is thus the weapon of faith. It is quite possible that if Christians had really acted in this way, while everyone else was thinking only of the material war (which *also* had to be waged), or of simply blessing the guns, the solution would not have been this terrible triumph of the Nazi spirit that we see everywhere in the world to-day.

The world of the present day is reaping what Christians have sown; confronted by a spiritual danger Christians called men to arms and fought with material weapons. We have conquered on the material level, but we have been spiritually defeated. Christians alone could wage the spiritual conflict: they did not do so. They did not play their part in the preservation of the world.

At the present time we see the same error being committed in the sphere of reconstruction. It is the duty of Christians, and of the Churches, to begin with work on the spiritual plane: a work which tries to understand the true situation of the world; an effort to understand and to proclaim the order of God; this implies an attempt to work out *Christian* 'reconstruction,' or an outline of the kind of civilization worthy of man;

all these activities are concrete possibilities for the Church. If this is not done, everything else is futile. Anything else will only create still more disorder.

It seems to me that this participation (which is both effective and specific) for the preservation of the world, can lead us to the idea of 'redeeming the time.' If we put two texts together from Colossians and Ephesians, in parallel columns, we shall see that they have been constructed in exactly the same *way*, and that Paul's train of thought is very clear:

Colossians 4.5–6	Ephesians 5.15–16–17
Walk in wisdom toward them that are without,	Look therefore carefully how ye walk, not as unwise, but as wise;
Redeeming the time.	Redeeming the time . . .
Let your speech be always with grace, seasoned with salt.	Understand what the will of the Lord is.

Without even trying to penetrate into the problem of 'redeeming the time' (that is, the notion of time which is enslaved, which must be redeemed in order to become free), we should only consider that we have here an astonishingly living suggestion for the study of the situation of the Christian in the world; a suggestion which seems to be at the very centre of this problem, because it is placed, as we might say, at the vital point, as a link between conduct and preaching, between good works, the fruit of wisdom, and the knowledge of the will of God. We then cannot avoid considering this notion of 'redeeming the time' owing to the fact that it appears in connexion with the situation of the Christian (and not from the theological point of view) at the centre of the Christian life, as being the particular and decisive function of the Christian, which includes all that we have said up till now. In any case, these two passages show us that there cannot be any separation between preaching and conduct, that to 'redeem the time' is both a work of preservation (and, indeed, a work of very genuine preservation) and a work of salvation, for here there is no more separation. Thus this situation of the Christian in the world appears to be singularly charged with meaning if we reflect that 'redeeming the time' depends on his conduct and his preaching (or simply on his witness).

But there is still another point to be considered if we are to grasp the concrete character of this situation. In order to participate truly in this preservation of the world, the Christian ought to place himself at the point of contact between two currents: the will of the Lord, and the will of the world.

The will of the Lord, which confronts us both as judgment and as pardon, as law and as grace, as commandment and as promise, is revealed to us in the Scriptures, illuminated by the Spirit of God. It has to be explained in contemporary terms, but in itself it does not vary. This revelation gives us the conditions in which the world can live, that is, exactly those in which it can be preserved. But this preservation cannot be realized *in itself*. Even if we combine all the conditions for this preservation, logical, physical, political, economic, even if we realize these conditions set us by God, all will be useless unless we are working for this preservation in the light of salvation. For God does not 'preserve' the world on one side, and 'save' it on the other. He preserves it by saving it, and he saves it by utilizing this preservation. The will to preserve, and the order of preservation, are the same as the will to save man, and the proclamation of the Gospel; but this needs to be incarnated in a real world, and our action, as well as our message, ought to be guided by the present situation of the world, without allowing this to modify either the content or the unity of this will of God.

The will of the world is always a will to death, a will to suicide. We must not accept this suicide, and we must so act that it cannot take place. So we must know what is the actual form of the world's will to suicide in order that we may oppose it, in order that we may know how, and in what direction, we ought to direct our efforts. The world is neither capable of preserving itself, nor is it capable of finding remedies for its spiritual situation (which controls the rest). It carries the weight of sin, it is the realm of Satan which leads it towards separation from God, and consequently towards death. That is all that it is able to do. Thus it is not for us to construct the City of God, to build up an 'order of God' within this world, without taking any notice of its suicidal tendencies. Our concern should be to place ourselves at the very point where this suicidal desire is most active, in the actual form it adopts, and to see how God's will of preservation can act in this given situation. If we want to avoid being completely abstract, we are then obliged to understand the depth, and the spiritual reality of the mortal tendency of this world; it is to this that we ought to direct all our efforts, and not to the false problems which the world raises, or to an unfortunate application of an 'order of God' which has become abstract; if we act thus we understand that the work of preaching necessarily accompanies all the work of changing material conditions.

Thus it is always by placing himself at this point of contact that the Christian can be truly 'present' in the world, and can carry on effective social or political work, by the grace of God.

In the following chapters we shall try to deal with some manifestations of this 'will to death' at the present time, and also with the Christian's attitude, when confronted by these facts.

II

REVOLUTIONARY
CHRISTIANITY

IN the present world situation the necessity for a profound change, for a radical transformation of our present civilization is realized by everyone; men call this change, 'revolution.' On the other hand, people live in such an atmosphere of constant movement, in such a whirlpool of ideas, of social forms, of events, and in so much uncertainty, that they are very fond of saying that the world of the present day is 'revolutionary.' Finally, so much seems to be going on: so many new solutions are proposed, and there are so many revolutionary parties, that people are persuaded that there never was a time when there were so many 'revolutionaries'! Thus, realizing that 'revolution' is necessary, they are convinced that it is already here. Since these impressions are widespread, it behoves us to examine our present situation more closely than ever before.

It is scarcely necessary to insist on the fact that revolution is needed. Our Western civilization has gained control of the whole world from the mechanical and rational point of view, but this has led to a fatal *impasse*. Disaster, in every possible form, has flooded the world to an extent never known before.

Totalitarian wars, dictatorships, famines administratively organized, the complete moral disintegration of social institutions (like the nation and the family), and of personal life (individual immorality), the fabulous growth of wealth, which does not help people at all, the enslavement of the greater part of humanity under the control of the State, or of individuals (capitalism), the de-personalization of man, both as a whole, and at particular points—all this is only too familiar.

Now man does not feel himself very happy in this situation. He has scarcely any security or hope left; he demands a change, and, indeed, a change is badly needed. Only the further we go, the more we perceive the inadequacy of human solutions, which all fail, one after another, and only increase the difficulties in which we are living. The further we go, the more progress we make, the more do we confess that we are incapable of dominating and directing the world which we have made; all of us, in spite of our desire to keep hope alive, are aware that this is true. All this only increases our desire to see a true change which would put things right.

Thus when we consider the troubles of our day, the impossibility of finding remedies, and the necessity for revolution, we are tempted to say that this world of ours is 'apocalyptic,' that it is the world of the Last Days. It is easy to treat this idea with irony, and to point out that at every period in history men have believed that their epoch was exceptional, dramatic, and final. Whether we think of the second century after Our Lord, or the year 1000, or the sixteenth century, this fact emerges again and again. Is there any sense in calling our epoch more troubled, more 'apocalyptic' than any other? Actually, this is only an optical illusion, and in two hundred years, when the details with which we are obsessed will have disappeared, our day will seem historic like others, and not 'apocalyptic' at all. We must not allow ourselves to be led astray by our passions and our illusions.

In answer to this argument we would say: that it is not our concern to evaluate objectively whether this period in which we are living is more or less unhappy than any in the past. What really matters, not in the eyes of the historian, but in those of man, is not the material objective reality itself, but the way in which men think about it, and the sufferings, the hopes, and the anxieties of these persons. It is not without reason that the 'man-in-the-street' to-day feels himself utterly helpless. That is what matters; further, as Christians, it is essential to understand that every moment of man's life is not historic but apocalyptic. If we take the Fall seriously, the expulsion from Eden, which implies the constant presence of death, and if we take seriously the promise of the return of Christ, of which we know neither the day nor the hour, we are obliged to consider the present moment as apocalyptic, that is to say as the 'last' before man is confronted by judgment and mercy. A Christian cannot have any other vision of the world in which he lives than an apocalyptic one; and, knowing very well that historically it is not necessarily the end of the world, he must act at every moment as if this moment were the last. That is why we are so often commanded to 'watch.' What matters is not the 'end of the world' as we know it, but life itself, which is really apocalyptic. Our world is 'apocalyptic' in this sense; but this does not alter the fact that this demand of all our contemporaries for a revolution, which they feel to be necessary, is fully justified.

Now, in spite of the conviction that our epoch is revolutionary, that men are revolutionary, we are forced to assert that beneath all this apparent movement, and apparent development, actually we are not moving at all. It is true, of course, that there is a great deal of disorder and violence, that there is progress in technics, that there are social and political experiences, but in reality our world is standing still, because its framework remains absolutely fixed; the development that has been accomplished has taken place in a perfectly logical, and not in a revolutionary way.

In point of fact there are a certain number of values and of forces which are of decisive importance in our world civilization: the primacy of production, the continual growth of the power of the State and the formation of the National State, the autonomous development of technics, etc. These, among others— far more than the ownership of the means of production, or any totalitarian doctrine—are the constitutive elements of the modern world. So long as these elements continue to be taken for granted, the world is standing still. At the present time all 'progress' consists in developing the framework of our civilization. All parties, whether revolutionary or conservative, liberal or socialist, of the Right or of the Left, agree to preserve these fundamental phenomena.

Indeed, how could it be otherwise since we are living in an era when there is an agreement between the facts and the sentiments of men? Since, for example, in every sphere of life there is technical progress, and at the same time men believe that this increasing technical skill will bring men the greatest possible good. Yet all the catastrophes which afflict our epoch are connected

with this framework. To prove this statement, long
and detailed studies would be required, which would
take us too far away from our present subject. For the
moment we will confine ourselves to this statement:
that the universal catastrophes of the present time are
not due to accident, or to 'bad luck,' nor are they
mere breakdowns in the happy mechanism of 'progress.'
They are the inevitable product of the essential structure
of our civilization.

Hence it is utterly useless to try to discover remedies
for our present distress without altering this framework.
Now, as we have already said, everyone accepts this
situation, the reality of which has never been fully seen
or understood. Thus it is futile to talk about 'revolution,' or to put it more exactly, if we do use the word,
it tends to be interpreted purely in Marxist terms. That
is, instead of a 'revolution' which reverses the logical
course of history, we have a 'revolution' which is the
climax of this process of logical development. Thus the
revolution which men look for is one which will greatly
strengthen the power of the State, which will increasingly subordinate man to his economic function,
leading to a more and more complete submergence of
the 'person' in a mass-civilization. Such a 'revolution'
would give us no hope of any change in the disastrous
results of the situation from which we are now suffering.
And, of course, *this* revolution is quite irrelevant for
the hopes of modern man.

What is more, we are forced to believe that every
other revolution is now impossible, because, in order to
succeed, a revolution would be obliged to use the
methods of the present world. For instance, in order to
set man free we would need the adhesion of numbers of
men, that is to say, the use of methods of propaganda

to which we are accustomed, and then our politics would have to be addressed to the masses, because this alone would actually succeed, and it would be useless to try to accomplish a revolution without this basis. But if we use mass methods, we become involved in the complexity of these institutions, and in order to 'liberate' man, people begin to destroy the actual liberty everyone still possesses. What is finally achieved is almost the equivalent of the 'choir of free men' in the book *Ubu enchainé*.[1]

Here is the whole drama of Communism and of Fascism. They are incapable of making a genuine revolution in our civilization because they accept the essential basis of this civilization, and confine themselves to moving along the lines of its internal development. Thus, utilizing what this world itself offers them, they become its slaves, although they think that they are transforming it. All the revolutions, advocated both by Communism and by Fascism, are superficial modifications, which change nothing in the real problem of our day.

This profound immobility, this incapacity for revolution—which is certainly the essential characteristic of our epoch—in opposition to the exasperated desire for this most necessary revolution, creates a formless kind of society. In spite of all the political struggles, which have never been so violent, in spite of apparent contradictions, there is a progress towards uniformity, an alignment of all values, of all ideologies, based upon a few essential elements of civilization.

[1] The reference here is to a book by Alfred Jarry (c. 1895). This writer created a character 'Le Père Ubu' who appears in several of his works. The 'Père Ubu' is the symbol of all the forces of tyranny and the arbitrary use of power which menace human life to-day. (Tr.)

I have no desire to deny these conflicts. They exist, but they are illusory. That is, the men who are struggling are fighting for illusions, and this is one of the dramatic elements of the present time. Incapable of really altering their condition, these men sacrifice themselves for bad reasons. The actual conflicts at the present time are not truly revolutionary: they are struggles of persons, of teams—struggles for power. The protagonists of these different parties enter into violent discussions about means (but the aims are not questioned); they represent opposing forces (but not different views of the world). Essentially, for instance, Communist society is based on the same facts as Capitalist society: and at bottom, the U.S.S.R. obey the same rules as the U.S.A. Man is no more free on the one side than on the other; he is simply used for production in different ways. Man is not more fully preserved on one side than on the other, only he belongs to a different section of mass-civilization. Justice is just as much flouted on the Right as on the Left, but for different reasons. Whether we live under a dictatorship or in a democracy the financial technique is always the same, just as the American rationalization of labour closely resembles that of the Stakhanov Movement.

Once the postulates of our civilization are admitted, appearances alone can change. Individual or State capitalism, Western or Eastern democracy, all these are different costumes worn by the same man—but 'it isn't the habit that makes the monk.' Yet it is on account of this habit that the men of our own day are summoned to kill each other, in order to achieve this revolution for which they long; yet the very conditions of their conflict prevent them from achieving it.

Now, however, we have the right to ask: 'What is
the general motive which—at the present time—leads
man to this blindness about the world in which he
lives?' There is no doubt that the most powerful
motive—which weighs upon us like an interdict, the
motive which prevents us from questioning the
elements of this civilization, and from starting on the
road leading to this necessary revolution—is our
respect for *facts*. It is well known that in other civilizations men did not respect facts to the same extent, nor
did they conceive facts in the same way. At the present
time the fact, whatever it is, the established fact, is
the final reason, the criterion of truth. All that is a
fact is justified, because it *is* a fact. People think that
they have no right to judge a fact—all they have to do
is to accept it.

Thus from the moment that technics, the State, or
production, are facts, we must worship them as facts,
and we must try to adapt ourselves to them. This is the
very heart of modern religion, the religion of the
established fact, the religion on which depend the
lesser religions of the dollar, race, or the proletariat,
which are only expressions of the great modern divinity,
the Moloch of fact. The procedure is always the same.
People take the fact—the 'proletariat,' or the fact—the
'State,' or the fact of 'money'; then they divinize it, and
it is suddenly imposed on a whole category of men,
without difficulty, because modern people are ready to
fall down and worship facts. Everyone takes it for
granted that fact and truth are one; and if God is no
longer regarded as true in our day it is because He does
not seem to be a fact. Now it is this kind of intimate
conviction which constitutes the religion of the masses.
To have a 'religion' there is no need of creeds and

dogmas, ceremonies and rites: all that is necessary is that men in the mass should adhere to it with their hearts. Now if we try to see what men as a whole worship in our day, it is easy to perceive that whatever form their worship may take, it is always connected with the 'fact.' We only need to look through illustrated magazines to see that this is so.

Anyone who questions the value of the fact draws down on himself the most severe reproaches of our day: he is a 'reactionary,' he wants to go back to the 'good old days,' and those who make these reproaches do not realize that such questioning is, perhaps, the only revolutionary attitude possible at the present time. Still, we ought to know by what authority we refuse to worship the fact; because the way of surrealism hardly seems adequate.

A striking example of this religious authority of the fact is provided for us by the atomic bomb. Confronted by this discovery, by this instrument of death, it was quite possible for man to refuse to use it, to refuse to accept this fact. But this question was never even raised. Mankind was confronted by a fact, and it felt obliged to accept it. All the questions which were raised after that were secondary: 'Who will use this weapon? How shall we organize its control? What will be the best thing for us to do with it? Shall we use it for destruction in war or for peace? How are we to organize our economy with it in view?' But no one ever raised the question: 'Is this line of action itself good or bad?' The reason is that 'the fact' itself at the present time seems to be something which is beyond good and evil. So that the questions which throng around a phenomenon like that of the atomic bomb are questions which arise out of *things*, from the fact—and impose

themselves upon man; they are not questions that
man asks himself, or which he imposes on the matter—
it is the atomic bomb which constrains man to think,
to move, to enquire; it is the problems evoked by the
existence of the bomb which seem to be the greatest:
that is to say, problems imposed by a fact. And these
are no longer the questions which man, 'because he
knows good and evil,' can raise about the very existence
of the atomic bomb, about the existence of a fact.
Thus man divests himself of his true dignity, and he who
should dominate things and the world becomes the
slave of 'facts'; this 'slavery' is more complete than that
which any intellectual dictatorship ever hoped to
achieve. Thus man, who wants to master the material
world, submits to the dominion of matter, as expressed
in the fact; henceforth his thought, his life, his sentiments are all under the control of experience, of the fact.

Now so far as our present discussion is concerned, it
is important to note that this submission to the fact is
the anti-revolutionary position *par excellence*. As between Creon and Antigone modern man would take the
side of Creon. The revolutionary act, to the extent in
which it enters into the struggle against the power of
the fact, is a desperate effort, but modern man no
longer fights against facts.

Proudhon, affirming the supremacy of the human
will over human conditions, calling man to struggle
against his situation, is revolutionary, while Marx, who
explains that inevitably, by the evolution of facts
(including the simple fact of man) by the play of
dialectical materialism, Socialist society will emerge
from Capitalist society, is anti-revolutionary. Socialism, in becoming scientific, that is to say, in submit-
ting to fact, and in following the development of facts,

has become anti-revolutionary. The worship of fact forces man to subordinate his will to the development of facts. So that when opposition to a fact actually emerges, it means that the opponent believes that the situation is about to alter, and that a new state of affairs is about to appear. Thus people prefer the fact of the future to a present fact which is losing ground, but this is not the affirmation of a truth; it is simply the statement of a result.

For ever since society came into existence, the revolutionary spirit, which is a necessary part of social life, has always been the affirmation of a spiritual truth against the error of the moment: a truth which is called to incarnate itself in society, not in any automatic, mechanical way, but by the desperate, sacrificial effort of man. He makes this superhuman effort for the sake of a hope which is beyond himself, by a supreme exercise of his free will, which he pits against all the constraints and conventions which surround him. This has always constituted the essence of a revolution, and we refuse to give another meaning to this term. Revolution is *not* the course of history; it may spring from it, it may put the clock back—but in no case does it simply follow the beaten track. There is a logical course of history; revolution consists in resisting this logical course (or dialectic) in the name of a truth and a liberty which are endangered by 'normal' development. If the revolution succeeds, later on people will say, 'that was the true course of history.' But that is an illusion of the historian. The combinations of social, political, and economic facts are always innumerable, and their solution is never strictly logical. It is the fact that man *chooses* one of these different solutions, which causes one to predominate, which is just as valuable (though not more so) than the others. This choice may be 'conformist': that is to say, it may be seen to be the obvious line to follow in the normal course of events, in the general line of development—or it may be 'revolutionary': that is to say, it will be a new truth, which has never yet become operative as a social force.

Thus, actually, the position of the supporters of political and economic liberalism, of the Capitalist system, and of classical democracy, are the supporters of the present fact, who are unaware of its course of development; they do not know that its influence is waning. History cannot be reversed. Thus their position is one of conformity to the past. The position of the supporters of Socialism (and principally in its extreme forms, National Socialism and Communism) is that of men who look back to the development of the last hundred years, and tend to pursue their course along the same line. They are just as much 'conformists' as the previous group, but they are 'conformists' of the future: and the reason why their doctrines are so popular is that the masses are 'conformist' by nature.

The revolutionary position is quite different. But we still have to ascertain what it is, for it cannot be merely the affirmation of 'truth' or of 'liberty,' or the affirmation of a new political doctrine: a revolutionary position is totalitarian. Now we ought to realize that if this revolution does not take place, we are 'done for,' and human civilization as a whole is impossible. At the present moment we are confronted by a choice: either, a mass civilization, technological, 'conformist' —the 'Brave New World' of Huxley—Hell organized upon earth for the bodily comfort of everybody—or, a different civilization, which we cannot yet describe

because we do not know what it will be; it still has to
be created, consciously, by men. If we do not know
what to choose, or, in other words, how to 'make a
revolution,' if we let ourselves drift along the stream of
history, without knowing it, we shall have chosen the
power of suicide, which is at the heart of the world.
But we cannot have many illusions; confronted by the
power of organization, our revolutionary knowledge
can scarcely be used. On the other hand, where are the
men, at the present time, who have a true sense of
'revolution'?

II

Now the situation of the Christian in the world is a
revolutionary situation. His share in the preservation
of the world is to be an inexhaustible revolutionary
force in the midst of the world. Here we are concerned
with the preservation of the world, for in our own day,
as I have tried to show already, 'conformity to history'
leads to catastrophe: to the death of millions of people:
to the disappearance of the possibilities of a human
civilization, to the technical establishment of suicide.
In order to preserve the world, it is actually necessary
that a genuine revolution should take place.

But when we say that the situation of the Christian is
revolutionary, and that it is here that the change in our
civilization must begin, this statement sounds para-
doxical and ironical. To say that the Christian is a
revolutionary, does not always seem obvious in history,
and it is not at all evident at the present time. For
to-day Christians certainly seem to be the most conservative, and, indeed, the mildest of men—and on
the other hand the theologians seem to be obliged to
be anti-revolutionary, since they teach respect for

authority, and that all authority comes from God. But the fact that Christians, as human beings, at certain periods in history lose sight of the revolutionary character of their religion, does not mean that the Holy Spirit has ceased to work, and that the *position* of the Christian, to the extent in which he confesses his faith in the world, has ceased to be revolutionary.

For the intervention of the Holy Spirit is not dependent on man and his choice, any more than the revolutionary character of the Christian situation depends on man. It is not because men choose Christ that they become Christian, it is because Christ has chosen them. It is not because Christians choose to go out into the world that they work there, it is because Christ sends them there. They are not revolutionary because they feel the urgent need for revolution; it is for another, independent, reason, which we shall have to examine later on. The situation of the Christian is revolutionary for other than intellectual or self-chosen reasons: it is revolutionary of necessity, and it cannot be otherwise so far as Christ is acting in his Church. This situation is part of the work of the Church in the world, and it is true to say (as a simple fact) that during the greater part of its history the Church has, indeed, been in a revolutionary situation.

We must, however, define what we mean more precisely: we are here concerned with a *situation*, but not necessarily with an *action*. This situation may be defined as 'a state of permanent revolution,' which *may* be translated into concerted action, but which may also remain in a state of ferment, and lead to a work which is slow and deep, just as revolutionary as a sudden outbreak—which may, indeed, be a climax, or a crisis, but not a thorough-going revolution. Our concern is for a revolution affecting the world, and not only the State, or the government. It is possible to have a 'conformist' attitude to the government, and yet to be revolutionary towards the world. Here the idea of revolution is much deeper. Here the concern is not essentially to change the form of the State, or of an economy, but the very framework of a civilization, which ought to be continually examined and tested. Evidently a change of this kind will lead indirectly to very deep political or economic changes, but it does not inevitably lead to a direct conflict with authority, unless the latter champions the disorder which exists, and openly challenges the truth of God with regard to a new order.

Thus, we have a deeper vision (even though only a preliminary one), of what this revolutionary character of the Christian Faith might be in the world at the present day. Now we must define the conditions and the consequences of this situation.

The first condition is a well-known truth, but its reality is not sufficiently understood: *the Christian belongs to two Cities.* He is in the world, and he has a social life. He is the citizen of a nation; he has a place in a family; he has a situation, and must work to earn money; the setting of his life is the same as that of other men; he lives with them; he shares with them the same nature and the same conditions. All that he does in this world, he ought to do seriously, because he is bound up with the life of other people, and must not neglect what are called 'duties,' since he is a man like everyone else. On the other hand, he cannot wholly belong to this world. For him this world can only be a 'tabernacle,'[1] in which he is a 'stranger and a pilgrim.'[2] For him it is a temporary situation, although extremely important, because he belongs to another City. He derives his thought from another source. He has another Master.

All this should be understood in the most strictly material sense: living in this world, he belongs to another: like a man of one nation who resides in another nation. A Chinese residing in France, thinks in his own terms, in his own tradition; he has his own criterion of judgment and of action; he is really a stranger and a foreigner: he is also a citizen of another State, and his loyalty is given to this State, and not to the country in which he is living. It is the same with the Christian, he is the citizen of another Kingdom, and it is thence that he derives his way of thinking, judging, and feeling. His heart and his thought are elsewhere. He is the subject of another State, he is the ambassador of this State upon earth;[3] that is to say, he ought to present the demands of his Master, he establishes a relation between the two, but he cannot take the side of this world. He stands up for the interests of his Master, as an ambassador champions the interests of his country. From another point of view (and here the relation is quite different), he may also be sent out as a spy. In fact, that may be the situation of the Christian: to work in secret, at the heart of the world, for his Lord; to prepare for his Lord's victory from within; to create a nucleus in this world, and to discover its secrets, in order that the Kingdom of God may break forth in splendour.[4] He may be in this world, it is true, but all

---

[1] 2 Pet. 1.13.   [2] Heb. 11.13.   [3] 2 Cor. 5.20.
[4] Cf. the spies who were sent into the land of Canaan (Josh. 2.1; Heb. 11.31).

his 'ties' are elsewhere; all his ties of thought, truth, and fidelity depend on his Lord, and he owes no allegiance to the world. Further, when we speak of 'this world,' we are referring to concrete realities: the nation, the State, the family, work. . . . To all this the Christian cannot swear an unconditional loyalty. His first duty is to be faithful to his Lord.[1]

Now the two Cities to which he belongs can never coincide, and the Christian must not abandon either the one or the other. He may long to return, by death, to his native city, to his own country, but so long as he is upon earth he cannot possibly renounce the one or the other; on the other hand, he cannot be satisfied with the fundamental dualism in which he is involved. In other words, that inner tension to which we alluded in Chapter I, re-appears at this point; here, however, it is expressed in the realities of social, political, and economic life. The Christian who is involved in the material history of this world, is involved in it as representing another order, another Master (than the 'prince of this world'), another claim (than that of the natural heart of man). Thus he is obliged to accept this tension, this opposition, and the results from the acceptance of this inner tension—because he knows that the two orders can never be equated with one another—that the opposition between this world and the Kingdom of God is a total one. But it is an intolerable situation, which causes acute suffering, and it is not a satsifying statement. The Christian can never regard himself as being on the winning side, nor can he look on with pleasure while everyone else 'goes to perdition'; should he do so, he would be lacking in the Spirit of Christ, and by that very fact he would cease to be a

[1] Matt. 10.37.

Christian. Bound up with the lives of other men (by economic and sociological laws, and also by the Will of God), he cannot accept the view that they will always remain in their anguish and their disorder, victims of tyranny and over-work, buoyed up only by a hope which seems unfounded. Thus he must plunge into social and political problems in order to have an influence on the world, not in the hope of making it a paradise, but simply in order to make it tolerable— not in order to diminish the opposition between this world and the Kingdom of God, but simply in order to modify the opposition between the disorder of this world and the order of preservation that God wills for it—not in order to 'bring in' the Kingdom of God, but in order that the Gospel may be proclaimed, that all men may *really* hear the good news of salvation, through the Death and Resurrection of Christ.

Thus there are three directions in which the Christian ought to act in the world: first of all, starting from the point at which God has revealed to him the truth about the human person, he must try to discover the social and political conditions, in which this person can live and develop in accordance with God's order.

Next, this person will develop within a certain framework which God has ordained for him. This is the order of preservation, without which man lacks his true setting. Man is not absolutely free in this sphere, any more than he is free in the physical or biological domain. There are certain limits which he cannot overstep without danger to the society to which he belongs. Thus the Christian must work, in order that the will of God may be incarnated in actual institutions and organisms. Finally, this order of preservation will only have meaning if it is directed towards the proclamation of salvation; therefore, social and political institutions need to be 'open,' that is, they must not claim to be all, or absolutes. Thus they must be constituted in such a way that they do not prevent man from hearing the Word of God. The Christian must be ceaselessly on the watch—intelligent and alert— to see that this 'order' is preserved.

But, in so doing, he will find that he is confronted by two possible errors. The one error consists in believing that by constant progress in this 'order' we shall attain the Kingdom of God. It is enough to remind ourselves of the Book of Revelation, or of Matthew 24, to condemn this attitude. The other error arises out of the conviction that by achieving certain reforms we shall have reached this order which God wills. In reality all solutions, all economic, political, and other achievements are temporary. At no moment can the Christian believe either in their perfection or in their permanence. They are always vitiated by the sin which infects them, by the setting in which they take place. Thus the Christian is constantly obliged to reiterate the claims of God, to re-establish this God-willed 'order,' in presence of an order which constantly tends towards disorder. In consequence of the claims which God is always making on the world the Christian finds himself, by that very fact, involved in a state of permanent revolution. Even when the institutions, the laws, the reforms which he has advocated have been achieved, even if society be re-organized according to his suggestions, he still has to be in opposition, he still must exact more, for the claim of God is as infinite as His forgiveness. Thus the Christian is called to question unceasingly all that man calls progress, discovery, facts, established results, reality, etc. He can never be satisfied with all this human labour, and in consequence he is always claiming that it should be transcended, or replaced by something else.

In his judgment he is guided by the Holy Spirit—he is making an essentially revolutionary act. If the Christian is not being revolutionary, then in some way or another he has been unfaithful to his calling in the world.

We have just seen that one of the elements which makes this condition necessary is the actual situation of the Christian in the world. But there is a second fact, still more significant—if that be possible—and that is the promise of the glorious return of Jesus Christ, the *Parousia*. The Christian is essentially a man who lives in expectation. This expectation is directed towards the return of the Lord which accompanies the end of time, the Judgment, and proclaims the Kingdom of God. Thus one who knows that he has been saved by Christ is not a man jealously and timidly attached to a past, however glorious it may be. He does not cling to the past of his Church (tradition), nor even to the past life of Jesus Christ (on which, however, the certainty of his faith depends)—but he is a man of the future, not of a temporal and logical future, but of the *eschaton*, of the coming break with this present world. Thus he looks forward to this moment, and for him all facts acquire their value in the light of the coming Kingdom of God, in the light of the Judgment, and the victory of God. This is true for all theological facts; just as the whole of the Old Testament cannot have its full meaning as the work of God save in the light of the Person of Christ; so is it also with the life of Christ: His message acquires its meaning through the Cross, and the Cross is only significant through the Resurrection, and the Resurrection is only illuminated by the Ascension (which proclaims that 'Jesus is Lord')—but we must not go too deeply into theology!

In any case this theological truth also applies to social and political facts. The actual events of our world only acquire their value in the light of the coming Kingdom of God. It is the imminence of the Return of Christ which gives genuine seriousness to each actual event, and, indeed, it is through this fact that each actual event acquires its true content. Without this direction history is an outbreak of madness. Now in this matter the Christian has no right to keep this truth to himself; by his action and by his thought it is his duty to bring this 'coming event' into the life of this present world. He has to carry into the actual world of the present day elements which belong to the *eschaton*. In so doing he fulfils a prophetic function, and as historians have observed, the prophets of Israel always had a political part to play, which, in connexion with their civilization, was genuinely revolutionary. Every Christian who has received the Holy Spirit is now a prophet of the Return of Christ, and by this very fact he has a revolutionary mission in politics: for the prophet is not one who confines himself to foretelling with more or less precision an event more or less distant; he is one who already 'lives' it, and already makes it actual and present in his own environment.

This then is the revolutionary situation: to be revolutionary is to judge the world by its present state, by actual facts, in the name of a truth which does not yet exist (but which is coming)—and it is to do so, because we believe this truth to be more genuine and

REVOLUTIONARY CHRISTIANITY 51

more real than the reality which surrounds us. Consequently it means bringing the future into the present
as an explosive force. It means believing that future
events are more important and truer than present
events; it means understanding the present in the
light of the future, dominating it by the future, in the
same way as the historian dominates the past. Henceforth the revolutionary act forms part of history: it is
going to create history, by inflecting it towards this
future, and this notion of revolution is valid for all
revolutions which have taken place in the course of
history, whether they were successful or not. It is still
true for the Communist movement, but, as we have
seen, the latter has abandoned its revolutionary line in
order to follow the main trend of historical development. Indeed, to direct this action towards a future
which seems most likely to be realized, and is the
logical outcome of present conditions, is certainly *not*
the way to achieve a revolution!

The Christian, on the contrary, even if he does not
make a great show politically, or a great demonstration
of revolutionary power, but if he really lives by the
power of Christ, if, by hope, he makes the coming of
the Kingdom actual, is a true revolutionary. He
judges the present time in virtue of a meta-historical
fact, and the incursion of this event into the present is
the only force capable of throwing off the dead weight
of social and political institutions which are gradually
crushing the life out of our present civilization. Here,
again, it is not a question of 'keeping an open mind'—
of choosing to do this or that, as though there were
various possibilities: it is the only possible attitude that
faith can adopt; to abandon this position would mean
ceasing to believe that we have been saved, for we are

saved by hope, through faith,[1] and hope is precisely this eschatological force in the present world.

Thus we have before us the two fundamental theological facts which make the Christian life necessarily revolutionary: truths which have not been created by the will of each individual but by the situation which God creates for his children; and we ought to be convinced that if we do not live in accordance with this vision we have no idea of what the Christian life really is. Now we must draw conclusions from this fact.

One of the first series of conclusions will doubtless appear very abstract and difficult! It consists in the fact that the Christian cannot judge, or act, or live according to 'principles,' but according to the reality, lived here and now, of the *eschaton*—the very opposite of an ethic.

We must be convinced that there are no such things as 'Christian principles.' There is the Person of Christ, who is the principle of everything. But if we wish to be faithful to Him, we cannot dream of reducing Christianity to a certain number of principles (though this is often done), the consequences of which can be logically deduced. This tendency to transform the work of the Living God into a philosophical doctrine is the constant temptation of theologians, and also of the faithful, and their greatest disloyalty when they transform the action of the Spirit which brings forth fruit in themselves into an ethic, a new law, into 'principles' which only have to be 'applied.' The Christian life does not spring from a 'cause,' but it moves towards an 'end'; it is this which

[1] Rom. 8, 24.

completely changes the outlook for humanity, and renders the Christian life different from every other life.

What is true in the individual sphere is also true in the social sphere. There are no Christian political and social principles, defined in an absolute way. What God reveals to us in this sphere by the Scriptures is not a doctrine or principles—it is judgment and action, wholly directed towards the accomplishment of the work of God. We never see a logical causal process, any more than we see the establishment of a static or a permanent order, but the action of God always appears as a power in movement, like a torrent which crosses and recrosses history, which changes its course, rolls along in great floods, and stirs up all the elements of creation. The Bible shows us a God at work in political and civil history, using the works of men and bringing them into His action for His promised Kingdom. From what the Scripture reveals to us about this action we can draw similar analogies, we can conceive the essential direction which our action should take. We can have a glimpse of a contemporary order with a changing shape, but not of a system, or of political principles. Whenever we have to transcribe the action of God in the world, in an incomplete manner, intelligible to humanity, there can be no question of any dogmatism, which is the very contrary of this action. Thus, the first consequence of this revolutionary function of the Christian is that he ought to be open to all human action, that he ought to welcome it as giving him valuable direction. We are never called to set aside a political or a social attempt on account of 'principles' which are supposed to be 'Christian.' Everything that seems to be a step in this right direction (in the sense in which this was defined above) should be most carefully examined.

On the other hand, it is evident that the Christian can never be tied to the past or to a principle. In the political world he must apply the rule of Ecclesiastes (Chapter III): 'To everything there is a season, a time to every purpose under the heaven. . . . He hath made everything beautiful in its time.' Thus there is not a Christian attitude which can be applied to all times, but according to different times, attitudes which appear to be contradictory, may be equally good, to the extent in which they make their mark on history as fidelity to the purpose of God. Thus it is not necessary to be loyal to an idea, to a doctrine, or to a political movement. What is called 'fidelity' in the language of the world is too often only habit or obstinacy. The Christian may belong to the Right or to the Left, he may be a Liberal or a Socialist, according to the times in which he lives, and according as the position of the one or the other seems to him more in harmony with the will of God at that particular time. These attitudes are contradictory, it is true, from the human point of view, but their unity consists in the search for the coming Kingdom. [It is in the light of this Kingdom that the Christian is called to judge present circumstances, and these circumstances cannot be judged according to their moral content or their individual political outlook —nor according to their relation to a human doctrine— nor according to their attachment to the past, but simply according to their relation, which always exists, to the *Parousia*.] There is no doubt that this is a difficult attitude, full of snares and dangers, but it is also the only attitude which seems to be in line with the

Christian life; we were never told that this would be either easy or secure.

The fact that almost all Christian political attitudes have been either wrong or disastrous (that of the Jesuits as well as that of Constantine, for instance) is due to the fact that judgment has been diverted from the Kingdom of God into a line governed by an ethical doctrine, and that people have always tried to construct 'a political system deduced from the Gospel'!

But, you will say, 'What do we know about this Kingdom of God?' In reality, we must take care that we do not make the Kingdom of God into an ethical system, by trying to outline the form in which it should be reproduced upon earth!

The central point which we can already know, and is already real, is the Lordship of Jesus Christ, and all Christian realism ought to be based upon this Lordship.[1] This Lordship is the objective element in the revolutionary Christian situation, as hope is its subjective element, and this alone permits us to take our stand in our different political positions, in our successive judgments on the concrete problems of politics and economics.

A thing is never good or bad in itself, not even by the use man makes of it. A thing is only good or bad in its own time, according to its situation in the light of the Kingdom of God, according to its conformity to the work of God for the coming of the Kingdom, and, finally, according to its possible use for the glory of God, or vice versa. These are the three criteria, which are very precise and concrete, once we have abandoned our obsession with ethical formulae or political doctrines.

[1] On Christian realism, see a detailed study by J. Ellul: *Réalisme politique et réalisme chrétien. Foi et Vie*, Nov., 1947.

It is in the daily application of these three criteria
to social facts that the action of the Christian is revolutionary, by 'actualizing the *eschaton*.'[1]

But we can see, quite easily, that this attitude goes
far beyond all current systems of idealism and realism.
The constant presence of the Kingdom in the Christian
life is a demand which urges one continually to go
further, to look at situations in their depth, and to make
still greater claims, for no revolution can fully satisfy,
and in the same way every achievement, however
humble it may be, is worthy of being preserved. Thus
we need to take account of all the facts, and to transcend
them; not, however, in a spirit of intellectual arrogance
or in the name of some abstract dogma. The vitality
of this realism is due to the fact that it judges nothing by
'effecting' a success; its only criterion is the Lordship
of Christ. Thus the Christian is called to 'judge all
things,'[2] an order which St. Paul gives in an absolute
manner. That is to say, it concerns the whole of life,
and not only 'moral values' or the 'spiritual life.' We
ought also to emphasize the point that in the text this
injunction appears in a passage between an exhortation
about prophecy and the reminder that the whole of the
Christian life has only one aim—to be preserved unto
the coming of our Lord Jesus Christ; and, in consequence, that this Pauline sequence of ideas is at the very
heart of all that we have been able to write here about
the revolutionary position of the Christian.

This judgment (which is not derived from human
rules or customs), which has to be ever new, and ever

---

[1] Or 'realizing the presence of the end' in daily life. (Tr.)
[2] I Thess. 5.2, 5.23 'Quench not the Spirit; despise not
prophesyings . . . and may your spirit, soul and body be
preserved . . . at the coming of our Lord Jesus Christ.'

renewed, is the very heart of the realist position of the Christian. I am quite aware of the possible criticisms which may be raised; how this may seem to denote a lack of unity, of continuity, of fidelity, and the like; but I believe that all this is due to a wrong Christian attitude, adapted far too much to the pagan idea of what this attitude ought to be. Nothing is more irritating than the way in which non-Christians use biblical phrases, which they do not understand, in order to criticize the attitude of Christians. The value of their criticism of Christians does not come from their knowledge of Scripture but from their way of living. Non-Christians are an example when they live differently from, and better than, Christians, on any particular point, but Christians have not to follow the intellectual or moral lessons or doctrines which the non-Christians may want to give them.[1] Now this equation of Christian thought and Christian ethics which has been an obvious fact for the last two hundred years, is the secularization of Christianity—by Christians themselves, with their lack of daring and of fidelity; and on this particular point the criticisms addressed to Christian realism are a manifestation of this attitude.

But this realism is not limited to daily facts. The principal question is raised, as we have seen, by the phenomenon of the internal framework of our civilization, which causes the catastrophes in the midst of which we are living, and, on the other hand, forbids all revolution. The Christian situation is essentially revolutionary, as we have said, and this ought to appear

[1] Luke 16.8.

in the life of the present day. It is true that church-
goers are no longer aware of this situation, and are very
little concerned about their mission on earth. This is
due to various causes, which it is not our business to
examine here. It is also true that the Churches have
proved to be lamentable ambassadors, and have failed
to play their revolutionary part. Instead of acting as a
ferment or a leaven in society, too often they have
either been immersed in the lowest form of politics, or
in a 'spirituality' which has lost touch with ordinary
life. But, willy-nilly, the man who confesses Jesus
Christ finds himself one day confronted by this responsibility. He is brought to a decision which shows that
his real position is revolutionary. Whether this decision
be conscious or not, it is still revolutionary by the very
fact that it is the decision of a man who acts for personal,
and not for sociological reasons. This is not common
to-day.

Having been led to study this problem, we do not
claim to be able to throw new light upon it. In this
book, I believe that I am simply describing what has
always been the situation of the Christian in the world.
To become aware of this situation is not a sign of
'progress,' it is even, in my opinion, the exact opposite.
In reality, the actual problem of revolution is a problem
of life or death for man, and it is presented to us to-day
in terms which we have never known before. Now no
one, unless he is moved by a supra-human power, can
consider himself truly revolutionary. All that belongs
to the world has become radically conservative, and
maintains the forces which inevitably lead towards
suicide. On the other hand, and at the same time,
Christians no longer act according to that unconscious
impulse which, whenever the Church was fully alive,

made them the bearers of a profound revolution. To-day this inner impulse seems to have faded away— and in spite of their faith Christians usually act as sociological beings. They seem to be unaware of their Christian freedom. Since they have ceased to be 'unconscious revolutionaries' it is high time that they should rouse themselves and take stock of their position: they need to realize that they have a special mission to fulfil, and that it is their absolute duty to be revolutionary. If they are no longer 'revolutionary' in their outlook, perhaps it is because they have lost their spiritual vitality. The remedy is in their own hands: they must turn to God, and ask Him to give them the power of His Holy Spirit; they must pray for this continually, asking God to guide them and to give them strength to act as He wills in the life of this world— that they may be His instruments for the changes men so sorely need. But this revolutionary force, which manifests itself in the facts of daily life, ought also to attack the fundamental questions of our own day. It ought to be applied to changing the internal framework of our civilization (which is something very different from the various forms of economic life), and it ought to go much further than our 'revolutionaries' who belong to political parties are prepared to go; for their efforts simply amount to an attempt to establish firmly a world with which we are only too familiar, and which is already out of date. How can this be done? It will be a long, slow work, entailing first of all *knowledge*, awareness of the world in which we are living, and do not know, because no one can say that we 'know' it as a result of statistics and questionnaires!

And then comes the question of *a style of life*. Christians ought to try to create a style of life which does not differentiate them from others, but yet permits them to escape from the stifling pressure of our present form of civilization. For it is not by the method of direct attack, by the effort to make spectacular changes, by trying to reconstruct the world as a whole, that we can achieve anything. The only successful way to attack these features of our modern civilization is to 'give them the slip,' to learn how to live on the edge of this totalitarian society, not simply rejecting it, but passing it through the sieve of God's judgment.

Finally, when communities with a 'style of life' of this kind have been established, possibly the first signs of *a new civilization* may begin to appear. At the present time, however, we are in no position to reflect on such possibilities, nor to be attracted by such prospects! The first step to take is to become aware of our world; or, in other words, to create a revolutionary situation. Until this first step is taken, everything else is Utopian, and it is quite useless for Christians to give exclusive attention to social or political questions. But, although this may seem to be only an intellectual and spiritual operation (actually it is more than this), it is a very difficult decision to take, because it is a decision which means breaking with the ways of the present world. What matters is whether Christians will dare to risk everything in order to fulfil their function in the world.

III

THE END AND
THE MEANS

WHEN we reflect on the possibilities of action in the world, whatever form this action may take, for instance, evangelization, or political action; when we reach the idea that the 'style of life' is to-day one of the most positive forms of revolutionary action; when, finally, we search for ways in which the faith of the Christian may be expressed, we are setting the problem of the end and the means. At the same time, as we ook at our own day, we soon become aware that this is a formula, which, whether directly or not, pre-occupies our contemporaries. If they are intellectuals, they study the question both at its heart, and in its repercussions, like Huxley. If they are not intellectuals they adopt a pragmatic attitude which implies an implicit decision in this respect. In reality, this question is absolutely central for our civilization, and the solution which is given risks being the decisive element in the decline of our civilization.

Thus, when we consider 'the end and the means' we find ourselves both in the sphere of consequences, springing out of our preceding study, and in the most important sphere of action in the modern world.

I

Our first point is extremely important: the problem of the end and the means is an ancient problem, but its form has altered, and it is now expressed in very different terms from those which were used in earlier days. To wish to study the question to-day from its philosophical angle, whether moral or metaphysical, to state and resolve the problem in eternal terms is to condemn oneself to understand nothing, in spite of apparent cleverness. In reality to-day the problem has been absolutely transformed; it is no longer a discussion between two conceptions of the relation between the end and the means (for instance, 'the end justifies the means' and 'just ends, just means'), for it is no longer expressed in philosophical terms, but in terms of facts, and of particular facts, which are peculiarly urgent: technical facts. Thus this question is a clue to the understanding of our own day; that is, if we can state it correctly it will help us to understand our own civilization. But in order to state it correctly we must look at it from its factual point of view, which has altered the very basis of the question; that is, it must be seen in the light of technics.

On the other hand, it will not do to give an abstract answer to the question. We have no use for merely abstract obligations. In reality, like the majority of questions of fact, which are raised by our civilization, this question does not imply an intellectual or a technical answer. For those who are concerned it implies a practical decision: one has to come down on one side or the other. It pre-supposes a life-decision on the part of those who are aware of the question. No longer is it a sort of game, giving an abstract response to an

abstract question, as in other civilizations, but it is a
concrete question of one's attitude to life. The error of
our makers of economic and political systems is that
they play a game which consists in giving an abstract
answer to a concrete question! How then is this question of the 'end and the means' stated at the present
time, and from what point of view?

The first great fact which emerges from our civilization is that to-day everything has become 'means.'
There is no longer an 'end'; we do not know whither
we are going. We have forgotten our collective ends,
and we possess great means: we set huge machines in
motion in order to arrive nowhere. The end (by this I
mean the collective end of civilization, for individuals
still have their own ends, for instance, to succeed in a
competition, or to get a higher salary, and the like) has
been effaced by the means. Thus *man*, who used to be
the end of this whole humanist system of means, *man*,
who is still proclaimed as an 'end' in political speeches,
has in reality himself become the 'means' of the very
means which ought to serve him: as, for instance, in
economics or the State. In order that economics
should be in a good condition, man submits to the
demands of an economic mechanism, becomes a total
producer, and puts all his powers at the disposal of
production. He becomes an obedient consumer, and
with his eyes shut he swallows everything that economics puts into his mouth. Thus, fully persuaded that
we are procuring the happiness of man, we are turning
him into an instrument of these modern gods, which
are our 'means.'
In all spheres the course of development has been

the same. For instance, we must make man happy. In order to make him happy we must give him plenty of goods to consume. In order to achieve this a considerable production has to be organized, and then our consumption must be adapted to our production. But it is a very complicated process, for there are human obstacles and technical obstacles: the latter are gradually overcome by research; while the former have to be overcome by subordinating man to the machine, to the division of labour, to publicity, to the use of his powers without limit. Thus, man himself, alive and concrete, the 'man-in-the-street,' is subjected to 'means' which are supposed to secure the happiness of 'man' in the abstract. The 'man' of the philosophers and the politicians, who does not exist, is the only result of this tremendous adventure which brings misery to the man of flesh and blood, and transforms him into a 'means.'

This process can be seen everywhere. Another example comes from science and technology. At first men felt it important to know the Truth; after the philosophers came the scientists. They elaborated their theories, while others applied them; these have been used first of all to prove the truth of these theories, and then for the use of man; from that moment science was lost. Gradually technical means became more important than the search for Truth. Science has had to become more and more effective for technical purposes, and now science is only significant in terms of technology. Its whole direction is towards applied science. It is at the service of means. It has become a means for the creation of more perfect means; and the abstraction called 'science,' to which homage is always paid, has replaced the search for Truth. This development is particularly evident in the United States of America and in the Soviet Union, but inevitably it is gradually penetrating the rest of the world.

Thus it is not difficult to see that the world is wholly given up to means. That which one hundred years ago was an 'end' has now become a 'means' in its turn, and even the 'means of means.' But a remembrance of it still lingers, because the situation is so bleak that it is difficult to accept, and people transfer the ends pursued into the sphere of the ideal, of the abstract, of Utopia. An excellent example of this in politics is provided by Communism. The latter has invented the most remarkable doctrine of political means that has ever been known. It is more elaborate than any other, but for what end? People will say, without doubt, for Communist society. But, says Lenin, 'it has not entered the head of any Socialist to promise the coming of the higher stage of Communism.' He adds that 'no one must ever promise this Communist society, nor even intend to introduce it, for in a general way it is impossible to introduce it.'[1] Thus we have an admirable political machine which carries on in the form of means (for the dictatorship of the proletariat is also a means), in order to achieve illusory and hypothetical ends. And in order to secure happiness for men in the future, the men of the present day are sacrificed.

This remarkable proliferation of means thus leads to making everything 'useful.' In our world everything has to serve, that is to say, to be a 'means.' Art and everything that is 'useless' has to give way to the necessity for 'utility.' Anything which does not serve some purpose must be eliminated or rejected, and in matters which concern men and women the same view

[1] Lenin: *The State and the Revolution.* Ch. V, para. 4.

prevails. This is what explains the practice of euthanasia (for old people and incurables) in the National Socialist State. Anyone who is not useful to the community must be put to death. To us this seems a barbarous practice, but it is simply the application of the universal predominance of means, and to the extent in which this fact is developed we may expect to see the introduction of this practice into the whole of civilization. Then it will be justified as being for the greater good of Man.

Further, as means increase, and as ends are relegated to the abstract, they become implicit and are no longer questioned. Everybody to-day is aware of the general aim of civilization, and it seems futile and old-fashioned to ask questions about it. Everybody has vague ideas about 'progress,' and it seems that this notion of progress might be capable of replacing the pursuit of ends. People think that whenever there is change there is progress, and in consequence we are increasingly approaching that very vague and hypothetical goal which was exploited with such romantic ecstasy in the nineteenth century.

No one is now concerned to question in what these ends consist, nor to see exactly in what direction we are going. No control is now possible, for the ends have disappeared, or they seem to have no connexion with means; it is the latter which now occupy the whole field of activity, the attention and the admiration of man. It is true that we still talk about 'happiness' or 'liberty' or 'justice,' but people no longer have any idea of the content of the phrases, nor of the conditions they require, and these empty phrases are only used in order to take measures which have no relation to these illusions. These ends, which have become implicit in the mind of man, and in his thought, no longer have any formative power: they are no longer creative. They are dead illusions, which are simply put among the properties of the contemporary theatre. It is impossible to take them seriously any longer, and no one would die for them. A man will die for his own well-being, or because he himself has already become a means: the means of a party, of a nation, of a class, and as a 'means' he is thrust into a battle which is being fought for no end. The heroism of a soldier in wartime, or of a workman in a strike, is in reality the heroism of a means which does not really know where it is going.

And these impotent ends are incapable of creating means. Until now, means were created for the sake of the end: now the end no longer inspires, for it is only a word, it is not even a myth. It no longer creates anything, and the mechanism of the creation of means is very different. The latter reproduce themselves mutually.

Just as the genius is no longer necessary for most technical discoveries, but when a certain state has been reached the next discovery follows almost inevitably; and just as genius is no longer necessary for the politician, but circumstances and technical means to-day tell him what. he ought to do, similarly, in all spheres, means produce the creation of new means. Here, in the order of industrial means, in the world of finance and politics, men are subject to a strict law of mechanical causality. Man hardly intervenes at all. New kinds of production appear because new machines have been created, or because men have discovered fresh ways of exploiting matter hitherto unknown. It seems to make no difference that man may not *need* these new products, that these new creations may be absolutely useless.

The means begets another means. The latter is applied, for 'why ever shouldn't it be applied'? 'Why should it be called useless'? What is necessary is an end to measure it by, but there is no end any longer, and this auto-production of means has a very remarkable result: it definitely confirms the absence of ends.

We have seen how the aim sought for has become implicit and abstract. Then, it has ceased to move. We still hold the ideas of 'happiness' or of 'liberty' of a hundred years ago, although in a debased and weakened form. Now the development of means makes these ends absurd!; for the means have destroyed the very possibility of reckoning with habitual ends. But people do not even realize that the means which are now being employed involve the negation of implicit ends. So they congratulate themselves every time a speed record has been achieved by an aeroplane, and people work very hard to try to go still faster, as if speed were a valid and sufficient aim in itself. But what is the use of gaining time like this?

Every time that a new remedy is discovered everybody is delighted, and people work harder than ever to extend the work of healing. But what is the use of the life which we take so much pains to conserve? What is the use of time? What is the value of life, since it is precisely by the use of these means in our civilization that time and life no longer have any meaning, that man really does not know what to do with his time, and that life is more absurd than ever, because the spiritual foundations of time and of life have been destroyed in the heart of man? Modern man having been dehumanized by means, having himself become a means —in spite of the fact that 'time' has been gained, and new methods of preserving human life have been discovered—is like a savage who has been given a very delicate and perfect machine which he does not know how to use.

Look, then, at this man, now deprived of his 'time' and of his 'life,' after people have tried so hard to make him earn his own living! No civilization has ever been so wasteful of the time of human beings, and of their lives. Immense forces are used to enable a man to gain a few seconds of time, yet whole days will be wasted by unemployment or by standing in queues outside a government office: both are the result of the exaggerated importance given to means.

All that science can do will be used to save one life, and then millions of men are massacred by bombs, or in concentration camps: both are products of the enormity of our means. Similar examples abound on all sides. For instance, take the question of social security: with great ability a huge administrative machine has been established in order to ensure social security for mankind—but why? For what purpose? For no time has been more uncertain than our own, and what is this miserable 'security' which is offered to men? Some millions of francs! at the cost of the insecurity due to financial, social, and economic crises, of wars and of revolutions, which, owing to our technical means, actually affect the lives of all: men, women, and children. In this terrible dance of means which have been unleashed, no one knows where we are going, the aim of life has been forgotten, the end has been left behind. Man has set out at tremendous speed—to go *nowhere*.

The second characteristic of this question, as we see it to-day, is that the means justifies itself. The days are over when men used to argue that 'the end justifies the means.' Of course, it is true that there are still theorists who support this idea, and who construct systems based upon it, like the Communists; or some moralists are still naïve enough to get excited about it, and they place the problem on the ethical level. But in reality all this is simply ideology, belonging to an epoch when man was master, spiritually and intellectually, of his means, when he could choose between different kinds of means, and when he used to choose that which seemed the best in order to attain his end, and if this 'means' was condemned on moral grounds it was allowed to be used on account of the elevation and the beauty of the 'end' in view. But these ideas went out, fifty years ago, and it is laughable to see politicians who think they are 'modern' and 'free from prejudice,' who adopt this rule as a principle of action. Facts have made the system out-of-date, the principle inapplicable, and the ideas useless.

In reality, to-day what justifies the means is the means itself, for in our day everything that 'succeeds,' everything that is effective, everything in itself 'efficient,' is justified. The means, by being applied, produces a result, and this result is judged by the simplest criteria, e.g. everything to which we can apply the adjective 'more,' that is, greater, quicker, more precise, etc. If we can do this, the means is declared to be good. Everything that succeeds is good, everything that fails is bad. Now technics infallibly teaches us to discern the means, the only means which contains within itself the most brilliant success. Technics always succeeds. All technical objectives (which are not ends, and we must be very careful not to confuse them in our minds) are necessarily attained by the most perfect technical means. Thus a political system of means will be triumphant. Thus the Communist economy, which is an economy entirely concentrated upon means, produces marvellous successes, and as long as it is thus concentrated it will continue to make swift progress (but during this time obviously man may starve!). In this way, too, the German army, a model of technical means, represents a certain type of 'success,' since it took four years to break it, though its opponents were four times more numerous. It is easy to find examples of this kind.

It is easy to explain the triumph of this kind of politics: the means having become technical, knows no limits. It can be applied quite indifferently to every kind of object, and knows no other rule than technical laws. It is subject to no judgment of values. It can only be an instrument which functions well. It is, of course, true that judgments of value (good or evil, just or unjust) are generally applied to the end and not to the means. Henceforth the technical process has got rid of every ideological or moral hindrance. It functions absolutely like a machine, without any external value to trouble the good order of the flywheels or the pistons. Sometimes technical results, like concentration camps, make the majority of men shudder with horror, but that is simply because these people were outside this sphere of technical means: a Russian Communist does not 'shudder' over the camps in Siberia, nor was a National Socialist in Germany horrified at the extermination camps. When these practices have become general, and we have all become used to the mechanism of these 'means,' no one will be surprised by them any longer.

This process of self-justification has a triple result: the first is that man is no longer to any extent master of his means. That is a statement often made, and the old legend of the 'magician's apprentice'[1] is repeated century after century. It is no use to insist upon it, but there is one aspect of this idea which is often neglected, namely, that man can no longer choose his means. He no longer has at his disposal a whole number of processes to obtain a result, among which he can choose at will. Technics chooses for him, and it chooses with a precision, an exactitude which man cannot attain. It shows him the only means which is truly effective, and after all, why should man refuse this means? Thus his responsibility for the use of means is eliminated: there is no choice. No doubt people will say that it is not so everywhere: 'Look at the spheres of medicine, politics, law, and economics. . . .' But these techniques are still in their infancy. In these spheres man still makes his own choice, because here the technical side is developing slowly. But technics is like a child who grows very fast, and we already know what it will look like when it reaches maturity. In a hundred years' time, in these spheres, man will have the best means, without any possible discussion; they will be the same everywhere, all over the world, and everyone will be at peace—R.I.P.

A second consequence is the extension of technics to all spheres of life. To the extent in which ends disappear, to the extent in which man no longer has the choice of means, but where one way alone offers itself to his desires for action, he applies technics to all objects. This fact (which we shall be considering again later on) is all the easier to achieve because technics is regarded as neutral. We are still clinging to the classic

---

[1] Who begins a process leading to consequences he cannot check. (Tr.)

conviction, very restful in our agitated world, refreshing in our inferno, that means do not signify much, that they are secondary in comparison with the very noble and very righteous ends at which we are supposed to be aiming, that they are negligible and neutral. A table is neutral—from the point of view of good and evil, a machine is neutral; consequently the organization of labour is neutral, and the same view is held of administration or of the technical side of propaganda. That being so, then flying bombs and concentration camps are neutral too! In reality, when we say that we regard technics as neutral, we really think, at bottom, that it is good. The very fact that it extends man's powers shows that technics is good. To-day the means are justified by the power which they give to man: that is the meaning of that self-justification of which I have just spoken. But, in reality, this discussion is becoming theological, and I cannot carry it further here. Here we can only note this intimate conviction of man which strengthens his tendency to activism.

And now comes a third consequence, namely, that all the ends proposed by man for the exclusive means placed at his disposal by technics are evidently useless or inadequate. The means no longer has any need of the end, from the moment that it is justified in advance, and that is what makes it so ridiculous and so tragic when people try to propose fresh ends for our technical civilization. By the very fact that it is technical it is impossible to assign to it any other ends. It goes on its way, the blind leading the blind, it goes where every step leads it, an implacable monster which nothing can stop. Idealists like Huxley claim to subordinate our means to a fresh end, and to choose the best because bad means vitiate the ends. These ideas are honourable and objectively true, but they are as out of place in our own day as it would be to fight against a tank with an axe of the Stone Age. The same applies when the Church searches for ends to offer to the technician: they are necessarily ineffective. The technician does not need any aims in his life; he is satisfied with the immediate success of the means. In fact, this is the main reason—decisive, unique, and profound—why the Church and Christianity have lost so much ground. If the Church no longer plays a great part in the world it is because of this new position of the problem of means.

And the fact that technics justifies itself has a theological root which I must indicate in passing: this is evidence. Genesis 3.6: 'And when the woman saw that the Tree was good for food, and that it was a delight to the eyes, and that the Tree was to be desired to make one wise—she took of the fruit and did eat.' The evidence is the means used by Satan to decide man to act, without having convinced him. You do not argue with 'evidence'; you do not argue with an aeroplane which flies at more than six hundred miles an hour, or with penicillin! And man *needs* such evidence, in order to give himself confidence! Here again, however, I must not enter into the sphere of theology. All I want to do is to study facts.

The third characteristic of the present problem of means is that they are totalitarian. Our civilization is wholly a civilization of means, and means affect all spheres of life. They respect nothing. This totalitarian reality may be considered from two points of view, one of which we have already briefly indicated.

First of all, means have become so exclusive that they

exclude everything which does not help their progress,
everything which is not suitable for their development.
On the one hand, then, the means destroys all that
threatens its development: thus technics will attack
and ruin successively the moral judgment (and in consequence morals as a whole); the humanism which
claims to subordinate all things to man (but technics
does not admit that it can be limited by the interests of
man), and all the activity in which man expresses himself freely for the disinterested pleasure in the activity
itself, for everything must be 'useful' (thus 'art for art's
sake' must be replaced by art for the use of the community or of the *régime*); and all spiritual awareness
(because it is essential that man should be blind, in
order that he may be a good slave of the means which
he creates). Technics will abolish the critical sense, in
order to be able to develop freely (as everyone thinks)
for the greater good of humanity. Thus in ancient
days men put out the eyes of nightingales in order to
make them sing better, and the means, rising tri-
umphantly on the ruins of human values, constructs its
own values, which will help it to ascend. All the new
values are aids, supports of the means, as, for instance,
the new type of myth. The State, the nation, the race,
the proletariat, labour; all that is presented to us
according to the different parties, as 'spiritual values,'
is in reality only the setting for the development of
technics, the illusion which is presented to man to make
him accept this desert, an illusion which hides from him
the terrifying sterility of the world in which he is
living.

However, at bottom these new myths have an effect
that is not sufficiently emphasized: they place the
spiritual at the service of means. They permit the use

of that which until then had seemed impossible to use in man (and, by this very fact, was rejected by Marxist realism). This is the great discovery of the United States of America, which uses Christianity as a factor in labour, then of the Fascist dictatorships, which utilized spiritual forces for the material power of the nation, and, finally, Communism seems to have understood this point, and in its turn begins to utilize myths of whatever kind they are, even Christian ones, for the dictatorship of the proletariat. This subordination of the spiritual to technical means is the great revolution, and in truth the only one which our day has been able to accomplish: that is to say, it is the final point which puts a stop to every possibility of revolution.

The second aspect of this totalitarianism of means is that gradually it extends its sphere to everything; not only are material objects subordinated to technics, but man also. The latter is no longer subject, he becomes in his turn the object of the forces which he has created. Man no longer seeks to know himself, in order that he may acquire self-mastery, but simply in order that he may be used. He is no longer concerned to discover his true 'image,' but to reduce it to the state of 'facsimile.' So psychological tactics are invented, and labour camps, propaganda, directed leisure; probably, too, in a few years we shall have developed breeding studs for human beings, and human vivisection. We have explained elsewhere the seemingly inevitable succession of events which has produced this condition. The autocracy of means invades the spiritual sphere: at the present time spiritual problems have become problems of 'the means to use.' It is sufficient here to point out a certain American conception of spiritual questions, worked out, for instance, in *Elmer Gantry* (by Sinclair Lewis). But all this inevitably denudes these spiritual means of all substance, and because man has become 'object,' and because the spiritual is classed among spiritual 'means,' existence no longer has any possible significance. Existentialism, the philosophy of our day, is right to remind us that our existence is what it is, but it is wrong to say that man is free to give a fresh meaning to his life. The irremediable triumph of means takes away all liberty from man along this line. Still, to believe in this angelic virtue of man means that we do not know either our own day, or ourselves.

II

We are caught in a trap. It is no use pretending to be 'deep,' and to talk loftily about the possession of inward liberty. If liberty cannot be expressed in my life it is an illusion. For a Christian this situation is appalling, for what we have been describing actually proves that at the present time it is impossible to live one's faith, to bear a genuine witness. Of course, it is obvious that it has always been impossible to live one's faith, and we easily comfort ourselves by saying that 'our day is no worse than any other,' and that 'our difficulties are just the same.' Well, that is just not true! It may have always been impossible to live one's faith, but that was due to inward causes: 'Woe unto me! for the good which I would I do not: but the evil which I would not, that I practise!' But to-day this difficulty is increased still further by external causes. In no other civilization has man been so totally repressed. He may have been the slave of hunger, of natural circumstances, or of another man: but he always managed to preserve a margin of freedom, sufficient to remain master of the greater part of his time, and to choose his own line, out of several possibilities.[1] All civilizations have imposed a certain amount of restriction, but they left man a large field for free and individual action. The Roman slave, the mediaeval serf, was freer, more personal, more socially human (I do not say 'happier,' from the material point of view) than the modern industrial worker or the Soviet Union official. Our civilization which claims to exert no restraint, tries to dominate man as a whole, and to confine him within narrow limits, where all his gestures, and his secret thoughts, will be controlled by the social machine. This represents the triumph of means. It is this new fact which hinders men from living the Christian Faith. Thus Christians ought to be fully aware of the fact that the witness and the action of the Christian have also become impossible, owing to these circumstances; he ought to know that unless he can break down this supremacy of means, it is 'all up' with the social aspect of Christianity, unless a miracle happens, and it will not be long before the personal aspect also will be attacked, for faith in Jesus Christ cannot live long in this rarefied air. We must break this dictatorship. Christians must enter into a conflict 'not against flesh and blood, but against the principalities, against the powers, against the world-rulers of this darkness.'[2] And they ought to know that this conflict, which is primarily spiritual, at least at first, is a life and death struggle. Rimbaud's phrase is more applicable than ever—'The spiritual conflict is as brutal as any battle in time of war!'

I am not going to speak here about what ought to be:

---

[1] Unfortunately our history books, which are stupidly full of the glory of the nineteenth century, take the opposite view, but it has become a current idea.

[2] Eph. 6.12.

this would be too platonic a procedure in such an urgent
discussion. Nor shall I suggest means of action,
opposing one form of technics to another. I will confine
myself to reminding you of a way, which is an ancient
Christian way, abandoned for the last two hundred
years, which moves in the opposite direction of the
triumphant path traced by modern technics.

The first truth which must be remembered, is that
for Christians there is no dissociation between the end
and the means. It is a Greek ethical idea which has
caused this division. The point from which we ought
to start is that in the work of God the end and the
means are identical. Thus when Jesus Christ is present
the Kingdom has 'come upon' us. This formula expresses very precisely the relation between the end and
the means. Jesus Christ in his Incarnation appears as
God's means, for the salvation of man and for the
establishment of the Kingdom of God, but where Jesus
Christ is, there also is this salvation and this kingdom.
Only this situation is the exact opposite of that which
we have described as being ours to-day: while our
civilization absorbs the end into the means, in the
action of God, the means only appears as the realized
presence of the end. The end, this Kingdom, which will
'come' at the end of time, is already present when the
divine means (the only, unique, Mediator) is present.
The whole action of God consists in realizing through
His means the end, which is His work. Whether this be
the Covenant, or the Law, or the Prophets, or the history or the wisdom of Israel: it is always the same act
of God which manifests this unity of end and means.
But it should be the same in all Christian life; for the

Christian also the end and the means are united in the same way; thus he is irrevocably committed to fight with all his might against our present enslavement to means. Above all he must have a different attitude. It is not his primary task to think out plans, programmes, methods of action and of achievement. When Christians do this (and there is an epidemic of this behaviour at the present time in the Church) it is simply an imitation of the world, which is doomed to defeat. What *we* can do is of no importance unless we can offer it with a 'good conscience toward God.'

In this situation it is not our instruments and our institutions which count, but *ourselves*, for it is ourselves who are God's instruments; so far as the Church and all its members are God's 'means' they ought to constitute that presence of the 'end' which is characteristic of the Kingdom. Thus we never have to look for an objective outside ourselves, which we try to attain by very great effort (all efforts are accomplished in Jesus Christ), but we, within ourselves, have to carry the objective for which the world has been created by God. Whether we will or no, whether this be regarded as pride or not, Christians are not in the same situation as others with regard to the end: they have received this end in themselves by the grace of God. They have to represent before the world this unity between end and means, authorized by Jesus Christ. For it is not man who establishes this end, as such, and achieves it, it is God who orders and arranges it and then brings it to pass. This completely reverses the attitude (so usual when one has finished a piece of work) of those who add, as a sort of precaution, that 'of course it is for God to make it fruitful,' or 'do what you ought to do and let what will happen,' or 'man proposes and God disposes,' etc.: all this is merely popular human wisdom, which tries to bring God in somewhere. In this attitude as a whole there is, in reality, a dissociation between the work of man and the work of God, between the means and the end. Such a view of life is radically anti-Christian, when it incites man to carry on his affairs, and then adds 'God' out of a sense of 'decency' belonging to another age. In reality, the opposite is true: we see that God establishes His end and that it is this which is represented by our means. The direction is reversed, and this is a fact of extraordinary practical importance —it is not an intellectual game.

It means, for instance, that we have not to strive and struggle in order that righteousness may reign upon the earth. We have to be 'just' or 'righteous' ourselves, bearers of righteousness. The Bible tells us that where there is a just man justice prevails. It is, of course, understood, that here the word 'just' means being 'justified' by Christ, and that is why justice prevails where there is a just man. This is because the just man lives by the justice of Christ. This justice is present, for it is this which makes him just. Thus justice is not a goal to attain, or a balance to be acquired, but it is the gift of God, free and inexplicable, which exists in our life so that our means are not intended to 'bring in' justice, but to 'manifest' it. Likewise we have not to force ourselves, with great effort and intelligence, to bring peace upon the earth—we have ourselves to *be* peaceful, for where there are peacemakers, peace reigns. And it is always the same idea which prevails: this creation by God of good aims, like peace—a living creation in Jesus Christ—which can only be *translated* through our means. Thus the principle of the Christian ethic begins here. We must search the

Scriptures for the way in which we ought to live, in order that the end, willed by God, should be present amongst men. The whole object of ethics is not to attain an end (and we know very well that for a genuine Christian ethic there is no such thing as a striving for holiness), but to manifest the gift which has been given us, the gift of grace and of peace, of love and of the Holy Spirit, that is, the very end pursued by God and miraculously present within us. Henceforth our human idea of means is absolutely overturned; its root of pride and of power has been cut away. The means is no longer called to 'achieve' anything. It is delivered from its uncertainty about the way to follow, and the success to be expected. We can easily give up the obsession with means, from which our time is suffering, and, in the Church, we must learn that it is not our possibilities which control our action, but it is God's end, present within us.

I know very well the kind of reproach that will be levelled at me when I say things like this. For instance, some people will say that this is an 'individualistic' outlook, or an 'individualistic' notion of action, whereas the (great and valuable) discovery of our day is that our action ought to be collective. Or again, that it means burdening the individual with problems which are outside his sphere and concern all men. Or again, it will be said that I am suggesting an individual solution to questions which are not individual, and that not only do they concern all men, but also that they are problems connected with institutions. Thus peace and justice are matters of political and social organization, and, in consequence, we must have adequate means; the problem should not be stated in terms of the individual conscience.

These arguments are not really valid. We are not concerned here with setting an 'individualistic' idea of action over against a 'collectivist' or an 'institutional' one. On the first point, it is enough to emphasize the fact that here we are not thinking of the individual but of *God*. We are not concerned about *our* peace or *our* justice, but about that which *God* gives. In consequence this whole idea of means is not concentrated on the individual but upon *God*, and by this very fact it is a collective idea, for it is God who creates the unity of this action, and it is God 'which worketh in you both to will and to work, for his good pleasure'; and as it is One God, alone, acting in us by One Spirit, the collective unity of these means is assured, not by our human means, but by the very unity of God Himself. Evidently the fact that this collectivity and unity *exist* in spite of our unbelief is too much for us to swallow.[1] For so long as we refuse to trust God, so long as we want to secure our *own* action, to make it rational, to take it into our own hands, to give it the character that *we* want, we are refusing to abandon the dilemma of the individual versus the collective, created by our preoccupation with *man*. It is only the action of *God* which will bring us out of this dilemma: the action of God, related to man personally, which is always a relation between man and God, but which—because God is the same for all—through God, is also collective. In this way the idea of means is freed from traditional categories.

On the second point, the attitude to be adopted to institutions, we must say that in the last resort the search for means acting on man indirectly, the search for the modification of institutions in order to change human

[1] Lit. 'our unbelief is disappointed.' (Tr.)

conditions, is hypocrisy or a lie. If we are horrified by the fact that we do not place the changing of institutions (property, distribution, administration, etc.) at the centre, it can only mean two things: either we are conscious Marxists, and do not believe in the existence of human *nature*, but only in the existence of a human *condition*, which can be wholly and radically modified by changing institutions: but that is the negation of the Creation; or, on the other hand, we are hypocrites, and we are refusing to state the problem of man in its fulness. We are refusing to look at the heart of man, and are simply considering his environment. We are turning our eyes away from the 'image' of man, in order that we may merely look at his 'setting,' and if, it is true, the setting may more or less enhance the value of the image, it is not true that it is that which gives it its value; and if we act thus it is because we refuse to be wholly comitted to this adventure.

This does not mean that the changing of institutions is not important, but only that this change cannot come first; and, in any case, the frenzied search for means, in order to change these institutions, a search in which we are participating to-day, is an error in the sight of God, and is absolutely futile. (There is no need to be a Christian to be able to see this.) Thus it is quite good to try to discover institutional reforms, on condition that this research is the product of our fundamental attitude, and that it is an expression, pure and simple, of the presence of the end in the world, and also that the change takes place through the living presence, in the contemporary world, of the end and of the judgment. A very simple example may be taken from one of the social reforms which has sprung from Christianity: slavery was gradually suppressed during the course of the third and the fourth centuries, not by decrees, nor by the direct condemnation of slavery by the Church, nor by individual Christians, but because the Christians of the day were so conscious of their equality with their slaves, since they were all, as Christians, looking for the Return of Christ. Since Christ was about to come, it seemed both useless and unjust to have slaves! Institutional reforms, therefore, ought to spring out of the faith of the Church, and not from the technical competence of a few experts, whether they be Christians or not.

But, if it be true that this end has to take such a place in the world; if it be true that this is the only possible focus for our epoch, this will cause an unprecedented upheaval among the enormous means that our civilization has been piling up. What does this really signify?

The first statement—which is obvious—is that our means are entirely unsuitable for the only end that matters; and that when we say that our means have no aim, this is the simple truth. It is impossible to synchronize these means and the only end; and, for this very reason, these means are absolutely useless. 'But,' people will say (and I am thinking of technicians who are offended by such 'confusion' of thought), 'you are mixing things up, which ought not to be mixed! We have never claimed that we could bring in the Kingdom of God by our efforts. Our means are adapted to immediate ends. You have not the right to condemn them in the name of the Return of Christ. There are two orders which are entirely different: there are spiritual values, with the Return of Christ at the End, and there are material values; or, again, there is the order of grace and the order of preservation. There is grace and the law,' and so on.

Well, we reject this refutation point-blank. First of all, because, in fact, the technicians have, indeed, claimed to make the Kingdom of God come upon earth: it is *this* that is implied by the idea of progress, so brilliantly illustrated by Victor Hugo, Renan, and some others! Further, this idea of 'progress' is in harmony with the theological doctrine which rejects the idea of the coming of the Kingdom in catastrophe, and believes that it will gradually appear, as humanity ascends towards God. No, it is *you* who are confused in your thinking, not we! Further, we reject these objections because it is wrong to separate the two orders matter and spirit, grace and the law, etc. In reality the two orders of preservation and of redemption are not separated, but they are integrated, the one in the other. All the actions of man are subject to the Lordship of Jesus Christ. The means are appointed for that unique end; but when we say that they are ineffective, this does not mean that they cannot bring in the Kingdom of God, rather it means this: human means (technical or otherwise) are unable to achieve their particular ends, because man has refused the reality of the unique and absolute end. Thus the science of economics will wholly fail to order economic life aright, because it assumes that economics is a closed sphere, not subject to the actual judgment of the Return of Christ. This may sound incredible, but it is the fruit of revelation: all technical achievements are useless, unless they are controlled, given their right position, and judged by the coming Kingdom of God.

Here is the second consequence: all the means at

our disposal, all these technical means which the modern world has created in its pride and its vanity— money, and mechanical force, and propaganda, the cinema and the press, comfort, or the means of communication, all this miserable pandemonium in the midst of which bewildered men do not know what to do, may be put in their right place, if they are set in the perspective of that end, already present in the means that God uses. This view does not imply that all these means of our present civilization must be abolished, nor is it an arbitrary transcendentalism, based on the power of the spirit of man, nor is it an optimistic view of the issue of this adventure, because we do not say that 'this ought to happen'—all we are trying to do is to lay down one essential condition which must be fulfilled if these means are finally to make human life possible.

But this presupposes an attitude which is resolutely hostile to political realism, an attitude in which means are judged, not in the name of moral rules, but in virtue of this actual presence of the end willed by God. If these means are to be really ordered in the light of this eschatological event, they must cease to be limitless in their demands, and subject to no authority higher than themselves. They must be judged, accepted, or rejected. It is not their intrinsic virtue, their quality as means, which counts; it is their eschatological content, their faculty of being integrated under the Lordship of Jesus Christ. They are not good or bad, they are called to enter into the Kingdom of Love, and they are able either to enter it or not. They are either inside or outside the gates of the Heavenly Jerusalem. Their glory may or may not be brought as tribute to the glory of God. Thus it is not an exterior and added quality to these means which we have to consider, it is their situation itself. Nor are we forced to consider their immediate goal, but their actual content; this means that we ought to regard them far less as 'means' to something, than as human activities.

This is where we have to take the largest step. We have seen how the work of God invites us to suppress the distinction between the end and the means, and how our action is no longer a means, save to the extent in which it expresses an act of God, the 'end' already present. And now we go a step further, and claim that no purely human activity—all this work of man, which to-day fills the field of our vision—is really a 'means' at all.

In reality it is no longer a means for anything; it is only an activity, and as an activity it is also subject to this conception of the means which the Christian Faith shows us. Only this activity is not mad and incoherent, as one might have the impression, on the contrary, it is perfectly ordered and arranged. It consists of all those efforts of modern man, but put in their right place, and divested of their vast significance. It is no longer true— in this fundamental unity of the end and the means, in this genuine function of the means—that all this production of modern civilization is the necessary condition of the happiness of man, the cause of progress, and so on. It is no longer in the increase of means that one may hope to discover at last a value and a virtue. The future of humanity does not depend on mechanical forces. Instead of a progress from the past towards the future it is a movement of the future which explains and informs the present, so that our technical discoveries are never anything more than temporary expedients which need to be put in their right place in the perspective of the Kingdom. But 'to put them in their right place' implies that there are secondary aims, limited to these instruments. They are of *some* use.

Thanks to this new relation between the end and the means, we can say exactly what they are called to do, and what we may expect of them: this is something very different, both from ends which are absorbed in means, and from philosophical ends which are not related to means. To some extent this means the application of a common standard to all these forces, a common standard which can be given, owing to their relation to the Lordship of Christ, which is already present. Thus we can search the Scriptures to try to discover what reforms are needed and how a temporary order of God can be set up in the world, on condition that we are aware of its relative value, and that the means to utilize these achievements are not ordered in view of this achievement and are not judged by it, but on the contrary are ordered for the Kingdom of God and judged by it. Thus we find the true direction for our activities, and the true relation between these activities and the secondary aims that we can propose to undertake.

But this attempt to place the means in their true situation, to give the right direction to human activity, is only one more ideology, ineffective and without value, unless it be accompanied by a much deeper transformation. Concretely, we see that unless the world can re-discover, by a spiritual revolution, an end which is both transcendent and present, an end whose presence can be perceived even in the secret world of technics, it is lost. Now we may search right through all philosophies, but Christianity alone offers a solution. It is easy to say this, but it does not change anything! A Christian ought to understand his responsibility in this adventure, for Christianity (and God) will not act *ipso facto* in this sense. This adventure is not the course of history, which will go on, whether we wish it or not. It may be realized, and it may *not* be realized. God may act, or He may not act, and when God wishes to act He ought to find instruments which are supple and obedient, ready for His use. We ought to remind ourselves constantly of the lesson given us in the Scriptures, that God rarely acts in a direct and transcendent manner; on the contrary, as a rule He chooses a human instrument to accomplish His work. Now in this work of God, which is actually decisive[1] will God find the men He needs? In other words, when we say that the revelation of God in Jesus Christ alone provides a valid solution of the present impossible problem of the end and the means, will it have vital consequences for the life of people who, at the present time, call themselves Christians? Is it anything more than a simple intellectual position?

In reality it is at this point that we resume the argument of the preceding chapter. Our attitude towards the problem of the end and the means leads us to take up a position which is wholly revolutionary; it is actually a radical change in the perspective of human life. For Christians the first 'consequence' of this new position is this: that what actually matters, in practice, is 'to be' and not 'to act.'

---

[1] This applies also to the purely spiritual sphere. For, in the last resort, must we remain in our present dilemma: where Jesus Christ is either excluded from the world by means, or is Himself made part of the life of the world, and thus becomes a means . . .?

Our world is entirely directed towards action. Everything is interpreted in terms of action, nothing is more beautiful than action, and people are always looking for slogans, programmes, ways of action; indeed, our world is so obsessed by activity, that it is in danger of losing its life. We know that the great slogan of all dictatorships is this—action for action's sake. This brings us back, once more, to the problem of the end and the means.

At the same time our world tends to eliminate, almost wholly, the life of the individual. By the formation of masses, by the artificial creation of myths, by standardizing our living, and so on, there is a general movement towards uniformity, which leads man more and more to forget himself as he is caught up in this general tendency of our mechanical civilization. A man who spends all his time in action, by that very fact ceases to live. A man who spends his days rushing about in his car for hours at a time, at a speed of sixty miles an hour, has the sensation of living on speed, of intense activity and of 'gaining time,' but actually a mental torpor creeps over him—he becomes less and less alive; more and more he is simply an automaton in a machine, he has reflexes and sensations it is true, but no judgment, and no awareness of anything beyond. In the perfect working of his engine he has lost his soul. Thus we are all suffering from a weakness which may become a serious disease.[1]

But if what we have been saying about Christianity is true: the necessity for the Christian to represent the end in actual life, the necessity to give the world a true perspective, the necessity to rediscover secondary aims for activity itself, all this presupposes that action is

[1] Lit.: 'from an *atony* which may become an *agony*.' (Tr.)

no longer master, and that what we need to do is to *live*, and to refuse to accept the methods of action proposed by the world.

The central problem which *to-day* confronts a Christian is *not* to know how to act, it is not to choose one method out of innumerable forms of action which the world suggests to us, it is not to act with, or against, or in another way. When we see the innumerable efforts for action that the Churches make, when we see all the dissertations and 'calls to action' and programmes, when we see, for instance, that in the political sphere Christians go no further than this ridiculous question: 'Are we to act for or against Communism?' When we see that everything that I have been saying on this subject will, in the end, lead to questions which I know only too well: 'Oh, so you're against the machine? You're against technics?' etc., or again, 'What must we do to change these conditions?' When we see all this, we cannot help being horrified at this miserable imitation of the world, of the works of the prince of this world.

Christians are so deeply imbued with the fundamental doctrines of this world that they no longer have any liberty of thought or of life. Yet, 'Ye were bought with a price; become not bond-servants of men.'[1] This is our present situation: to be 'bond-servants' of men means to accept the fundamental outlook of the world, to share its prejudices and its reactions. We have lost the meaning of true action, which is the testimony of a profound life, action which comes from the heart, which is the product of faith, and not of a myth, or of propaganda, or of Mammon! What matters is to *live*, and not to act. In this world, this is a revolutionary

[1] I Cor. 7.23.

attitude, for the world only desires (utilitarian) action, and has no desire for *life* at all. We cannot exaggerate the significance of the fact of being spiritually alive. We must cease to believe that life depends only on vitamins, hormones, and physical culture. We must get rid of the idea of 'the sound mind in the sound body,' which is only another way of getting rid of 'life' for the sake of 'action.'

That men should be *alive*, instead of being obsessed with action: it is at this point that means can be put in their right place. But to do this evidently means a complete break with all the tendencies of contemporary thought. What, however, does it really mean 'to be alive'? This involves a certain quality of intellectual life which we shall be studying in the next chapter. But above all it is a fact of spiritual life. To be alive means the total situation of man as he is confronted by God; this is precisely what our world wants to forget, and wants to make us forget. It does this in many ways: in its philosophies and its thought, as, for instance, in materialism, spiritualism, surrealism, existentialism, essentialism; as well as in its concrete action, of which we have already said enough. In all spheres of human life, there is an immense effort to prevent man from entering this total situation where he is alive.

What is this 'spiritual life' which is 'life indeed'? It means to live by truths of the catechism whose living depths we can never fathom: Man created in the Image of God; judged and condemned by Divine justice; pardoned and saved by His love; a creature, unique and irreplaceable (man has become unique because the Son of God has died for each of his creatures; because each soul is called to Christian liberty, in a life of holiness, and thus rediscovers a life which is truly

'free,' because it is lived to the glory of the Creator)
called to be renewed in his mind, and to bear within
himself the truth of God: 'Know ye not that your body
is a temple of the Holy Ghost?'[1] Called to judge all
things, for 'we shall judge angels,'[2] and to participate
in the glorious coming of the Lord of lords. All this
comes from the life of the Holy Spirit within us: 'We
know that we have passed out of death into life.'[3]
There *is* no other life; but we must *live* it, and we must
not allow ourselves to be dried up by the influence of
the spirit of this world.

What hinders us is that we can only conceive this
action in the rational form of mechanical means. We
no longer conceive it in the form which is constantly
suggested in the Scriptures: the corn which *grows*, the
leaven at work within the bread, the light which
banishes the darkness. . . . Yet it is *this* kind of action
which we can really have, because this is how the Holy
Spirit works. Thus it is the fact of *living*, with all its
consequence, with all that it involves, which is the
revolutionary act *par excellence*; at the same time this is
the solution of the problem of the end and the means.
In a civilization which has lost the meaning of life, the
most useful thing a Christian can do is to *live*, and life,
understood from the point of view of faith, has an
extraordinary explosive force. We are not aware of it,
because we only believe in 'efficiency,' and life is not
efficient. But this life alone can break the illusions of
the modern world by showing everyone the utter
powerlessness of a mechanistic view.

In conclusion, once more I would remind you that
when I speak of 'life' I am not thinking of some esoteric
mysticism or vitalistic theory of hermetic philosophy. I

---

[1] 1 Cor. 6.19.   [2] 1 Cor. 6.3.   [3] 1 John 3.14.

simply mean the expression of the Holy Spirit, working within us, expressing himself in our actual life, through our words, our habits, and our decisions. Thus what we need is to rediscover all that the fulness of personal life means for a man standing on his own feet in the midst of the world, who re-discovers his neighbour because he himself has been found by God. In the powerful presence of the Holy Spirit we receive the answer to this work of God, and we are bewildered because we are no longer very sure about the way forward, which no longer depends upon us. The end, as well as the means, has been taken away from us, and we hesitate as we look at this way which lies open before us, whose end we cannot see; we have only one certainty, and that is the promise which has been made to us of a certain order, which God guarantees: 'Seek ye first His Kingdom and His righteousness, and all these things shall be added unto you.'[1]

To sum up: all that we have been saying about the end and the means, about the eschatological character of the union between the end and the means, about the fact that results do not depend upon us, about the necessity for life and not for action: all this is only the interpretation and the application of this saying of Jesus.

To-day we ourselves can only live in dependence on that promise, that actually 'all these things' will be given us, in addition to the Kingdom, which is both promised and granted to us.

[1] Matt. 6.33.

IV

THE PROBLEM OF
COMMUNICATION

THIS title may sound enigmatic to those who are
not used to an intellectual vocabulary. In reality
the question here raised is very simple. It deals with
the situation and the work of the Christian intellectual.
But, people will say: 'What has that got to do with the
function of the Christian layman in the modern world?
Are not intellectuals members of the Church like other
people, neither more nor less? Do they think that they
are so superior after all that St. Paul has said in condemnation of the wisdom of this world?[1] And, on the
other hand, are we not already overwhelmed by the
work of the intellectuals, especially in all this new
theology which is so intellectual?'

It is quite true that the Christian intellectual is a
layman, like other people in the Church. But it is also
true that inevitably, as an intellectual, he has a some-
what peculiar function to fulfil, both in the world, and
in the Church. He cannot help thinking in theological
terms, because his vocation as an intellectual impels
him to think out his faith; but he need not be a
specialist in theology, for he is a layman. It is not his

[1] I Cor. 1.2.

task to study speculative theology, but because his
work involves him in the life of the world, in the
activities of the world, he has to evolve some kind of
practical theology. He must think out, very clearly, his
situation as a Christian at work in the world, and he
must think out his faith in its relation with the world.
Thus, he has a very clear function to fulfil, and no one
can take his place. Further, in this decadent civilization
in which we are now living, the Christian intellectual
has a very special mission to the world, and we must
try to define it here. Our task, in effect, is to consider
the layman's presence in the *world*, and not the part he
plays within the Church; so for the moment let us
shelve all problems connected with Christian culture
or 'professional theology,' if I may so describe it!

But in the objection to intellectuals which I mentioned
above, there is one further point to be emphasized: it is
true that the intellectual is on the same level as all other
members of the Church, and I also admit that it is
wrong to make theology too intellectual (but may not
this objection also be due to the fact that the Christian
public has forgotten how to *think*?). Nevertheless, we
must not go so far as to suggest that God condemns
intelligence. This is not a defence of intelligence, but
simply a remark to help us to see the situation clearly.
'Be not fashioned according to this world: but be ye
transformed by the renewing of your mind . . . that
ye may prove what is . . . the perfect will of God
. . .'[1] If ye were 'taught in Him, . . . as truth is
in Jesus . . . that ye be renewed in the spirit of your
mind.'[2] It would be easy to quote other passages, but
these are sufficient to show:

(1) *That faith produces a renewal of intelligence.* But

[1] Rom. 12.2.   [2] Eph. 4.21–23.

what does this mean, if it does not mean a transformation of our ways of understanding, of looking at facts, of the very process of argument? The Christian intellectual can no longer have—I do not say the same philosophy, but—the same understanding of things and of the world, and of their reality, and of man himself. He can no longer grasp them in the same way, nor see them in the same light. But when we come down to brass tacks, what does this actually mean? This is what every Christian intellectual should try to find out in his work.

(2) *That this transformation relates to the present period in which we are living:* it is the point at which the Christian view comes into conflict with the spirit of 'this present age'; indeed, it seems to be the decisive point at which this separation takes place: it is because we can no longer understand things in the same way, because our intelligence is transformed, that conformity to the present world breaks down. This shows that the work of intellectuals in the Church is very important; through this break with the world they 'educate' their fellow-Christians. Is this, perhaps, the special work of the theologians?

(3) *That this transformation takes place in Jesus Christ, through the action of the Holy Spirit.* Thus it is not only an intellectual process (and that is what I wanted to say when I suggested that we are not here concerned with another philosophy), but a transformation of life, expressed in intellectual terms. Thus, it is the Holy Spirit who henceforth inspires our minds, and enables us to discover new ways of thought, and a new understanding of the world in which we live.

(4) *That the aim of this transformation is that we may discern the will of God,* particularly in the ethical sphere,

since our text speaks to us of that which is 'good,
acceptable, and perfect.' Hence it means a comprehension, not of the abstract or general will of God, nor of
the nature of God, but of His will for the world—a
will which acts in the midst of men, and, on the other
hand, of that which man can and ought to do in this
world in order to live according to the will of God.

I

In the sphere of the intellectual life, the major fact of
our day is a sort of refusal, unconscious but widespread,
to become aware of reality. Man does not want to see
himself in the real situation which the world constitutes
for him. He refuses to see what it is that really constitutes our world. This is true, especially for intellectuals,
but it is also true of all the people of our day, and of our
civilization as a whole. It is as though we were confronted by an enormous machine, equipped to prevent
man from becoming aware, from driving him into a
corner, to an unconscious refusal, or to a flight into the
unreal. The dramatic characteristic of this epoch, in
this sphere, is that man no longer grasps anything but
shadows. He believes in these shadows, he lives in
them, and dies for them. Reality disappears, the reality
of man for himself, and the reality of the facts which
surround him.[1]

The man of the twentieth century (and we may say
that is the first time in the course of history that this

[1] We do not intend here to touch the philosophical problem
of 'appearance' and 'reality.' We do not aspire to know whether
matter has reality, or whether all the visible world is simply an
illusion to our senses, if man can grasp a reality or if the myth is a
reality, etc. We are on a much more elementary level, and the
object of this enquiry will come out clearly as we go on.

fact appears) oscillates unceasingly between the phenomenon and the explanatory myth: that is to say,
between two 'shadows,' both of which are extremes, and
are opposed to each other. The phenomenon might be
described as the external presentation of the fact. Our
contemporaries only see the presentations which are
given them by the press, the radio, propaganda, and
publicity. The man of the present day does not believe
in his own experiences, in his own judgment, in his own
thought: he leaves all that to what he sees in print or
hears on the wireless.[1] In his eyes, a fact becomes true
when he has read an account of it in the paper, and he
measures its importance by the size of the headlines!
What he himself has seen does not count, if it has not
been officially interpreted, if there is not a crowd of
people who share his opinion. This statement, which
may seem over-simplified, is in reality at the basis of
all propaganda. A fact is untrue, it is printed in a
newspaper with a circulation of a million, a thousand
people know that the fact is false, but nine hundred and
ninety-nine thousand believe it to be true. Thus the
fact becomes true. That is what I mean by 'phenomena' or 'shadows' that the modern man grasps and
knows *exclusively*. Why exclusively? Because every day
he himself has a number—a very limited number,
perhaps—of genuine experiences, but he is so embedded
in his habits, that he doesn't even know it! On the
other hand, every day he learns a thousand things from
his newspaper and his wireless, and very important,
very sensational things. Can he help it, that his little
personal experiences, which deal, perhaps, with the
excellence of a plum or of a razor blade, are drowned in

[1] Cf. *Combat* (A. Robin), article on 'Expertise de la Fausse
Parole.'

this flood of important illusions concerning the atomic bomb, the fate of Germany, strikes, and the like. Now, these are facts of which he will never know the reality.

And it is these 'shadows' which become his life and his thought. This produces a result, very important from the intellectual point of view, namely, that modern man, submerged by this flood of images which he cannot verify, is utterly unable to master them. They are not co-ordinated, for news succeeds news without ceasing. For instance, in the columns of the newspaper he will read one day about an affair which quickly disappears from the paper, and also from the brain of the reader. It is replaced by others; it is forgotten. A man gets used to living like this, without a present and without a past. He gets used to living in complete incoherence, because all his intellectual activity is taken up with these fugitive visions, themselves without a past and without a future, and without any substance even in the present.

Now in this reality, real facts, within the reach of everyone, are entirely hidden, they have no outward reality, so of course they do not exist: for instance, social classes (save class dictatorship), the great city, or problems of transport (except in questions of town-planning). Attention is given to the fact which is of no great importance: the incident, whether political, military or economic, whether it be related to democratic organization or to the success of the Blue or the Red Army, or the United Nations, or nationalization: all these different incidents, by the way in which we colour them, are objects of human passions.

On the other hand, man evidently needs a certain coherence. He cannot submit to being simply an eye which registers, without understanding, the jerky images of a mad kaleidoscope. Man needs some logical connexion, he demands that there should be some coherence between all these surface facts. Now this cannot be their real coherence, for this would presuppose a true knowledge of the facts, and not only the superficial view that we have of them, and it presupposes a highly trained and alert intelligence. Now the more that the press and propaganda develop along their own lines, the more they appeal to the crowd, and the smaller the proportion of intellectuals becomes, the more it becomes necessary to simplify, and to present news and ideas in a very condensed way. It is equally urgent to give the explanation, the link between all these incidents: this explanation, and this link, however, must be on the level of the 'average' reader, a level which automatically sinks lower and lower.

This leads us to the other pole of our extraordinary present intellectual situation: the explanatory myth. In addition to its political character, and its mystical and spiritual necessities, the 'explanatory myth' is the real support of our whole intellectual system. It has often been considered an accident, something which only belongs to dictatorial régimes, but in reality it is the essential element in every kind of politics at the present time, and in our own sphere. Confronted by the confusion of these various phenomena, and the necessity to give them some coherence, they are linked together, from a purely external point of view, by a new phenomenon, which makes it possible to explain the rest. This phenomenon, which has a spiritual root, and is only accepted by an absolutely blind credulity, becomes the intellectual key which serves to open all secrets, to interpret all facts and to understand what is happening in the tempest of phenomena. We all know these explanatory myths: the bourgeois myth of the Hand of Moscow, the Socialist myth of the Two Hundred Families, the Fascist myth of the Jews, the Communist myth of the anti-revolutionary saboteur, etc., etc. But what is evidently very serious is that modern man has no other means of intellectual coherence or of political investigation than this myth. If he abandons it, he cuts himself off from the world in which he is living; he can, of course, simply lead his personal life; but this is a suicidal solution, for modern man cannot contract out of the world that we have made.

This myth, which we only mention in passing, and do not analyse completely, is, further, the stable point in the thought and consciousness of our contemporaries. Thus it is not only the means of understanding and of coherence: it is also the only element which seems fixed in the midst of streams of facts; this helps man to avoid the fatigue of thinking for himself, the disquiet of doubt and of being questioned, the uncertainty of understanding, and the torture of a bad conscience. What a prodigious economy of time and of means, which one can use to great advantage in order to produce a few more flying bombs! Modern man has a good conscience because he has an answer for everything; whatever happens to him, and whatever he does, depends on the explanation which is provided for him by the myth. But this process lands him in the most complete unreality. He lives in a perpetual dream, but it is a realist's dream, woven out of innumerable facts and theories in which he believes with all his might, as a man involved in a mass-civilization, who could not break away from the masses without dying.

What is the reason for this situation, from which it seems impossible to escape? There are a whole number of facts which combine to explain it: first of all, there is the really extraordinary complexity of our world. The more we advance and the more this world is formed of complicated organisms overlapping one another, variable in quality, but all seeming equally important—the more impossible it is to know them all, or to grasp them—so mankind wanders uncertainly through this forest.

Then there is the influence of the means of knowledge, placed at our disposal in order that we may meet these facts. These means (mainly the press, the radio, and the cinema) are essentially mechanical in their nature, and presuppose considerable capital in order to be put into action. In consequence they are obliged to depend on capital, whether that of private ownership or of the State. These two aspects of the means produce the following consequences in the order of political or economic knowledge: their mechanical character means that they can only be attached to the external aspect of facts. There are things 'which it is possible to represent technically on the radio, but others are impossible.' This means that we can only know one aspect. This twofold condition consequently leads to a mechanical choice among the actual facts. We have to find that which corresponds to the demands of the means—and, finally, the mechanical aspect means that we have to use large affirmations without any shades of meaning—and they have to be affirmations, not reasoning, for by the very fact that this has to be done by mechanical means, we are speaking to the crowd. The financial obligation of the means brings with it a certain restriction in choice of the facts which are to be broadcast. The presentation of an aspect of the world based upon hidden presuppositions, and the progressive application of these means to all spheres and to all men, since it is a condition that the affair should yield a high rate of interest (financially, if we are concerned with 'private information,' politically, if we are concerned with 'secrets of State'—it is all the same!).

A third element of explanation comes from the crushing character of the means of knowledge which society puts at our disposal. We can scarcely deny the information which is thus transmitted to us, and even if we doubt it personally this does not hinder the adhesion of the crowd, which is evoked by the evidence of power. There is no discussion with the radio or with the press. Their power over the masses is absolutely irresistible when it is employed in certain conditions (which specialized institutions make it their business to control more and more fully).

Finally, evidently we must take into account the question of 'distraction,' in the sense in which Pascal uses the word. To-day everyone is 'distracted' by civilization; indeed, we might say that our whole civilization, from its games and sports up to its serious business, has arranged everything in order to achieve this distraction. This is what I meant when I spoke about 'the effort to make men become unaware.' His way of life, his amusements, his work, his political parties, etc., all this absorbs modern man to such an extent that he easily falls a prey to these ways of acquiring information. Their influence is strengthened

by the man who uses them, who is profoundly incapable
of meditation and of reflection. He is satisfied with
these phenomena, with these apparent explanations,
because he is already 'distracted,' even before 'the
news-reel' or the wireless have helped to 'distract' him
still further. Thus the intellectual situation of modern
man is extremely serious; although he knows more
'things,' and possesses more mechanical methods, than
ever before, and although in theory he may be more
fully developed than at any other period in history,
this development is due to inaccurate information and
hazy facts.

But, someone may object, 'this is not the position of
the modern intellectual, though it may be that of the
man-in-the-street; that's all!' But actually the intellectual is also affected by the same atmosphere,
although in a different way.

The intellectual can easily see through the stupidity
of the explanatory myths. He can refuse to accept
them, and he can reject the terrible over-simplification
and the wretched dogmatism of the present time. But
when he has got rid of all this he is absolutely defenceless
when confronted by the mass of news which reaches
him from every quarter. He is capable, it is true, of
rejecting the myth, but he is not capable of attaining
reality. Thus in the current intellectual system, which
circles round an axis passing through the two poles—
the 'phenomenon' and the 'myth'—he is obliged to
preserve one of these poles, the phenomenon, and this
makes his thought wholly unbalanced. He is obliged
to adopt this position because the phenomenon does not
depend upon himself. But this intellectual may be
perfectly well aware that in so doing he is only concerned with an illusion. He can be perfectly clear of

the unreality of what others believe to be facts, but he still cannot grasp this reality. What then will he do? For some the solution is (intellectual) suicide: such people shut their eyes, and accept the myth, in order to remain in fellowship with the majority; they accept this sophism: 'Doubtless the phenomenon and the myth do not correspond to the facts, but the moment that men believe that they do, they become real, and we must adhere to this reality.' This is the great paradox of Communist and Fascist intellectuals (it is true that in this camp there were not many of them!). They have to commit intellectual suicide, and to abandon clarity of thought, in order to find a reason for existing at all! The intellectual will then adorn his 'suicide' with an intellectual crown, by appealing to the myth in which he believes: such as the permanence of man, or the dialectic of history.

Other intellectuals also commit suicide. The 'phenomenon' is so crushing and so pervasive—it becomes so impossible to gain a true view of political reality, or of the social and human reality of our day, and human development is so superficial that anyone who understands it despairs of ever knowing anything else, or of finding any kind of coherence in this perpetual motion. Thus the intellectual is gradually led to think that there is no reality behind appearances, or that, if there is one, it is entirely out of reach, and that, so far as man is concerned, it is absurd. Henceforth it is useless to look for an explanation, or for coherence, since we are wandering in a world of shadows. And because everything presents itself to our understanding in the form of appearance, because everything has already been interpreted, since the intellectual cannot know the reality of these facts, he refuses to accept any fact as valid and certain. Thus he comes to lose awareness of the world in which he is living. The result of this attitude will show itself in different ways, sometimes in a desperate heroism, sometimes in a surrealist dilettantism, but in any case it is intellectual suicide due to the despair provoked by the factual situation.

Whether directly or indirectly, all modern intellectuals adopt one or other of these positions. This comes out very clearly in the case of the Parisian intelligentsia. Thus the position of the intellectual is not particularly enviable. It is more precarious in our own day, when there are so many 'openings,' when novelists make such fortunes (but what novelists!), and when cultivated men and technicians are needed more than ever. This precarious situation is not due to material conditions, but to the intellectual and spiritual conditions in which the intellectual has to practise his profession. That is to say, he is menaced from within and no longer from without. However we cannot dwell on this point here.

We have considered one of the aspects of the intellectual transformation of our own time. There is, however, another, which is no less serious.

Until now the intelligence had various ways of expressing itself and of controlling the world and men. In our own day, however, the intelligence has found a form of expression which corresponds to our civilization, and one which presents new and disquieting features: it is technics. Owing to the fact that technics has invaded all spheres of action, we find it also in the sphere of intelligence. It goes without saying that we use this term 'technics' in its most comprehensive sense.

By it we mean literary technics (this has been more fully developed than ever, *cf.* Faulkner), technics in the realm of sociology, law, and history, and not only in the realm of science. All the spheres of intelligence are, in fact, exploited by the technicians. This, of course, has the advantages which are always presented by technics, of precision, rapidity, certainty, continuity, universality: which are all characteristics of efficiency.

This does not mean that technics is anti-intellectual. We might easily put it the other way round and say 'intelligence has become technical.' It is no use moaning about this situation, but we must be aware of it. Here as elsewhere technics is an instrument at the disposal of the intelligence, but after our study of the end and the means this idea is not very reassuring, and it must be admitted that this instrument has had a disintegrating effect upon modern intelligence.

It is striking that technics appears to be an instrument of our intelligence which is univocal. Whether we are concerned with intellectual matters or with the control of the world, or with self-knowledge, in all these operations there is a technical way, and this way, since it is swifter, more effective, and more practical, is the only way which a modern intellectual can use. There is no longer a choice. An entomologist will not act any longer like Fabre, nor an historian like Commynes. For there are precise techniques which give much better results, and if we do not use them we are regarded as amateurs, if not as humbugs! In point of fact, we might say that to-day the technical way is the only method which the intellect uses to express itself truly. This comes out very clearly in art itself, whether directly as in the cinema, or indirectly, as in modern painting, which is actually controlled by the obsession of 'self-expression,' and the effort to be as different as possible from photography—that is, a technical problem. Now this instrument—which the intelligence can modify, bend, and apparently control—this instrument which excludes any other, actually causes profound alterations in intellectual behaviour. It becomes imperious. The intelligence *may* manifest itself by intuition, but it does so in the abstract, it cannot coincide with this instrument which is so remarkably exact. This 'imperialistic' attitude of technics can be understood, for instance, if we look at the attitude of our modern intellectuals when confronted by the knowledge of the world, ways of acting on the world . . . proceeding from other intellectual methods, like those of the Indians or the Tibetans: the latter seem, to the modern intellectual, to be an object for research, and for sociology, but not as an intellectual path which is still open, another way leading towards the knowledge of reality and of truth. Only a few fanatics (usually Anglo-Saxons) try to follow this 'way' mystically. It is evident that this way of knowledge does not compete with our technics. This is only one example.

But so far as the intelligence is tied to its technical expression, so far as the intellectual tends to become a technician, his sphere of action—which seemed to be extended by all the technical aids—in reality becomes narrower and narrower. Because the intelligence cannot be freed from its instrument, it remains limited to-day to the sphere in which this instrument can act, can be utilized.

It we are not prejudiced already we ought to consider that according to current opinion there is a 'serious intellectualism,' one which can be used—

technics—and an intellectualism of fantasy, which no one takes seriously, which has no repercussions in any sphere, that is, one which does not succeed in being 'technical' because its object is not suited to this method —as, for instance, theology, metaphysics, and, in general, art.

This is simply the restriction of the intelligence owing to its univocal modern method. It is rationalism, not in the current sense, but in the sense given it, for instance, by a man like M. de Corte. Owing to this, the intelligence is forced to act on that which can be seen, weighed, counted, and measured. It acts strictly in the sphere of the material world, and tends to deny the existence of any other. And that which might have been simply the fact of a materialist theory, is now the result (which is more serious) of the very method of the intelligence. It is more serious, because a doctrine can be refuted, but one cannot question the technical method. The intelligence of modern man is no longer nourished at the source of contemplation, of awareness of reality, and is more and more absorbed by the instrument which it has created, an instrument whose principal aim is the control of the material world.

Thus the intellectual who takes his profession seriously can no longer be anything other than materialist, not theoretically, but owing to the methods which he uses. If there are other philosophical positions, these will have no effect on his actions, save to question his technical method—which is evidently catastrophic— not, perhaps, catastrophic from the genuinely intellectual point of view, but from the point of view of achievement, and of his personal career (for this intellectual will cease to be taken seriously).

So far as the intellectual is concerned, who imagines

that he can remain truly idealistic and humanist in outlook while employing the rational technique, his want of lucidity proves that he is not a true intellectual. Action which is entirely directed towards the material world, by eliminating its spiritual elements, in the last resort necessarily destroys this spiritual reality which lies at the heart of intelligence. The latter has become more and more the slave of its method, and can no longer find a way of escape. That which ought to be the liberation of the intelligence is the worst slavery that it has ever known—set free from dogmas it is the slave of means. There is no longer any conflict or tension between Ariel and Caliban. Caliban has produced a system where Ariel in chains finds his whole *raison d'être*, and caresses his chains with joy, under the illusion that he possesses a power which is in reality the very one Caliban possesses.

There evidently have been some reactions, sometimes violent ones; for instance, Cubism and Surrealism, which seek by means of the intelligence to gain an influence over the world by a way that is not technical. But what vitiates these reactions is, first of all, the fact that these movements deny the existence of a reality other than apparent phenomena, and refuse to admit an objective reality. This produces the first stage of intellectual degradation of our time. And, further, as soon as these movements were born, from an explosion, they had to look after their 'efficiency,' so they had to adapt themselves to the law of the present day, and they started looking for new techniques. This comes out very clearly in the sphere of Surrealism, and in the quarrels between surrealist factions. We thus perceive that they were led to an application of strict rules, forming a different style, but presenting the same fundamental features; strict rules, which are in reality technical rules excluding intellectual liberty.

These two facts which we have just emphasized—the lack of awareness and the enslavement of the intelligence to technical methods—lead, when combined, to the most terrible situation for the intellectual: absence of communication.

It is a platitude to say that the men of our day no longer understand each other. This is nothing new since the Tower of Babel. But God had left a certain relation between men through the intelligence. Now it is this bridge which our day has just broken down. Men no longer understand each other: on the level of the peasant this is not evident; on the bourgeois level it is inconvenient, on the intellectual level it is tragic, because, for the intellectual there is no other genuine reason for living than that of communication, in order to understand the world. To-day this communication has become practically impossible. In order to understand each other we need a minimum of ideas which are common and valid for everyone, of prejudices and values which are the same for all—and most often unconscious.

Now the mechanism of information increasingly destroys this common basis of communication. Doubtless, other prejudices are created, other common ideas which have other features: instead of being the expression, the most deep and the most authentic, of a certain kind of civilization, they are now the myths and the artificial ideas created by propaganda. This means that individuals can no longer meet one another in a given trend of civilization. They can only meet in each the myth in which they themselves believe, and this myth is only an artificial creation (we must come back to this again and again) created in order to prevent modern man from going mad.

Further, we have seen how the sense of reality—objective reality—is increasingly being lost, and the man whom we meet has ceased also to have for us an objective reality. We are more and more plunged into this abstraction, and this not only with regard to facts, but with regard to men. We can no longer communicate with man, because the man by whom we are faced has lost for us his reality. The intellectual of the present day no longer believes in the possibility of rejoining this man. He speaks in an emptiness and a desert, or, when he speaks, he speaks for the proletarian, for the Nazi, for the intellectual, etc. There never was a time when people have talked so much *about* Man: there never was a time when so little has been said *to* Man. The reason for this is that people know that it is futile to speak to him. Conditions are such that 'man' has disappeared. He remains in the form of the consumer, the workman, the citizen, the reader, the partisan, the producer, or the bourgeois. Some people wave the tricolour and others are internationalists, but in all this, man as man has disappeared, yet it is to him alone that one can really speak: it is with him alone that one can communicate.

Finally, we can no longer communicate with man, because the only intellectual method of expression is a technical one. The fact that the intelligence is obliged to use the technical channel breaks personal relations, because there is no possibility of contact between two human beings along this line. Communication transcends technics because it can only take place where

two human beings are fully engaged in a real con-
versation. Now this is precisely what the intellectual technique of the present day both avoids and
prevents.

The modern intellectual is aware of this great impossibility—and it is his very existence which is at
stake; what matters is to know definitely whether he
still has something to say to man which man can understand, instead of discoursing indefinitely about matter,
and how to perfect one's means; and this also concerns
the intellectual who calls himself Christian. The
modern intellectual seeks for ways—for instance, De
Rougemont with his search for a thought which
'commits' you, or Malraux, who re-discovers man in
'the Event.' This is not false, but it is ineffective. For
to say that man finds himself in 'the Event,' as, for
instance, in war, in revolution, in the concentration
camp, is tantamount to saying that he can only find
himself in exceptional situations, which in relation to
our civilization are very demanding, and, indeed, only
to the extent in which he escapes from our civilization.
But this attempt does not reach the heart of the problem, because it springs, necessarily, from a sphere
which is temporary, limited, and changing. This
physical or spiritual adventure, which is so necessary if
communication is to become possible once more, is only
itself the expression of this communication already
realized. It is impossible to recreate what has been
broken from the outside. It is impossible to re-discover
man artificially and in the exceptional elements of life.
Our *whole* civilization needs to be examined, and by
each person, on the plane of his individual destiny,
which may not be heroic, but which is certainly a
human destiny, and cannot exist without genuine

communication with the human beings by whom he is surrounded.

Here we also come upon one of the characteristics of our day: the 'will-to-death,' one of the forms of universal suicide towards which Satan is gradually leading man. Satan makes people gradually get used to this idea of suicide: suicide in enjoyment or in despair, intellectual or moral suicide and thus people are ready for the total suicide which is slowly preparing, and will involve the whole world, body and soul.

It is our duty to react against this habit of suicide in all its forms: the form of non-communication is particularly pernicious, particularly invisible, for the men of our day, when they want to meet one another, put their trust in the post office, the railway or the newspaper —that is to say, precisely in that which breaks and kills the very power of finding each other as human beings, in the reality of flesh and blood.

'See, I have set before thee this day life and good, and death and evil; in that I command thee this day to love the Lord thy God, to walk in His ways . . . I call heaven and earth to witness against you this day, that I have set before thee life and death, the blessing and the curse: therefore choose life, that thou mayest live, thou and thy seed: to love the Lord thy God.'[1]

'We give Thee thanks, O Lord God, the Almighty, which art and which wast; because Thou hast taken Thy great power, and didst reign. And the nations were wroth, and Thy wrath came, and the time of the dead to be judged, and the time to give their reward to Thy servants the prophets, and to the saints, and to

[1] Deut. 30.15ff.

them that fear Thy Name, the small and the great; and to destroy them that destroy the earth.'[1]

II

It is evidently an artificial idea to imagine that we can find solutions in a good theology. It is not by the application of principles, or by intellectual knowledge, that we shall put an end to this impossible situation of the intellectual, who is torn in pieces between his mission and its means, between his comprehension and the absence of communication. No human action can attain this. Once again, it is a question of *life*, and the problem of the incarnation of the intelligence is not gratuitous or superfluous: it is a necessity of our day, but it can only be by superhuman action that this human effort will find its meaning. In all that I am now going to say we shall find ourselves confronted by a logical impossibility. We are going to clash with the sphere reserved for God. We are pulled up sharply by the fact that all human action is only effective if it is filled with the fulness that God gives it—that it only accomplishes anything if God gives it the power to do so. This is the point, however, at which we must get rid of a confusion of thought which may have been produced by what I said in the first two chapters: we must not believe that the relations between God and man with regard to this necessary action are constructed thus: man does one part of the work, and God does the rest. ('Help yourself and Heaven will help you.') In reality, man does his work and God gives its meaning to this work, its value, its effectiveness, its weight, its truth, its justice—its life—and if God does not give this, let there be no illusion: let us not hope that the work of

[1] Rev. 11.17-18.

man will nevertheless subsist with a lesser value and a lesser truth: nothing remains of the work of man. It is dead; it fades into nothingness.

This is why, in all that we have said about this work which is so necessary in our present civilization, there is a breach which cannot be closed, an 'undermining' which cannot be avoided, and by which the power of God may (or may not) be manifested—a necessary action, but it is useless if God does not transform it by the gift of His grace, which is free and cannot be predicted.

To imagine that we can give men methods and solutions without leaving this breach, that we can do works which ensure their own efficaciousness, this is to do anti-Christian work, even if this work be inspired by the Gospel. Evidently our attitude leaves man hungry and thirsty, but it is because he refuses to drink the living water of which it is said that he who drinks it will never thirst again. This dilemma will come out more and more poignantly at this point.

The first duty of a Christian intellectual to-day is the duty of awareness: that is to say, the duty of understanding the world and oneself, inseparably connected and inseparably condemned, in their reality. This means the refusal to accept appearances at their face value, and of information for information's sake, the refusal of the abstract phenomenon, the refusal of the illusion given by present means, the consoling illusion of 'progress,' and of the improvement of situations and of men, by a sort of benevolent fatalism of history.

The first act, the first necessity, for this awareness, is a fierce and passionate destruction of myths, of intellectual out-moded doctrines (e.g. Liberalism,

Fascism, Communism, for instance, in the political sphere), it is the shattering of this intellectual bourgeois outlook which is 'conformism' in thought, whether to a dogma (as in Russia), or to a way of life (as in the United States); it is the violent break with this pageant of information and of 'news,' and the deflation, by a strict exegesis, of interpretations and 'balloons' which people try to present to us as capable of elevating the world. But in the name of what is this offer made?

The second element in awareness is the will to find objective reality, to discover the facts of the life led by the people who surround me. This is the creation of genuine realism, such as I tried to describe in my work on political realism already quoted: but here, again, we are obliged to ask the question: 'In the name of what?'

The third element consists in the fact that this reality ought to be grasped first of all on the human level. We must refuse energetically to be detached from this sphere, a level which is not very high, but is the only significant one. This means that first of all we must get rid of evasion, in all its forms, in the ideal, in the future, in abstraction. We must no longer think of 'men' in the abstract, but of my neighbour Mario. It is in the concrete life of this man, which I can easily know, that I see the real repercussions of the machine, of the press, of political discourses and of the administration. If people say: 'It all depends on whether we are looking at a farmer in Texas, or a farmer in the Soviet Union'—I don't know anything about this (and I won't learn that from newspaper reports), but I think I am right, because I believe in human nature.

I refuse to believe in the 'progress' of humanity, when I see from year to year the lowering of standards among men I know, whose lives I follow, in the midst of whom I live—when I see how they lose their sense of responsibility, their seriousness in work, their recognition of a true authority, their desire for a decent life —when I see them weighed down by anxiety about what the great ones of the earth are plotting, by the fear which penetrates our world, by the hatred which they feel for a terrible phantom which they cannot even name; when I see them cornered by circumstances, and, as they suffer, becoming thieves and frauds, embittered, avaricious, selfish, unbelieving, full of resistance and rancour, or when I see them engaged in a desperate struggle, which comes from the depths of their being, against something they do not know. The intellectual who wants to do his work properly must to-day go back to the starting-point: the man whom he knows, and first of all to himself. It is at this level, and at no other, that he ought to begin to think about the world situation.

If he wants to know what the cinema is, let him go to the cinema—not to see a work of art, or anything of that sort, but in order to taste life—that is to say, to enter into fellowship with this mass of spectators, to see them rather than the film, to share their feelings and their emotions—then he will know what a destructive power the cinema possesses over man, which does not detract from its other virtues. Evidently, this process of 'becoming aware,' which has nothing intellectual about it, pre-supposes that we can put up with anything, and are ready to risk a few sleepless nights. But when an intellectual can really do this he will have entered upon the path which leads to the real struggle for the life of the intelligence.

All other knowledge of the world, through statistics

or news, is illusory, and keeps us tied to the outlook we have been discussing.

The fourth element in this awareness consists in looking at present problems as profoundly as possible, to see them as they are, with, on the one hand, the implacable ways of our world, and, on the other hand, the situation in which we, as men, are placed. It is for us to find, behind the facts presented to us, the reality on which they are based; thus behind the various aspects of propaganda, this reality, common to all countries and all states, which is propaganda itself, apart from its sentimental or ideological content, without any real importance. We have to find, behind the theories which splash us and blind us from every quarter, the reality which they hide from us. For instance, behind the democratic or totalitarian aspects, the reality of the life of the technician, which goes its own way, whatever the setting may be. What we need is to find the true structure or framework of our modern civilization, though in order to get down to this we may have to do a great deal of difficult and delicate scraping away of extraneous matter. We need to understand this framework as the expression of the spiritual reality of our civilization, our present expression of the spiritual reality of the world. But this process of awareness of civilization should not be in any way objective. This brings us to the final element in awareness. It should imply an 'engagement' (or act of resolute committal).

The intellectual who does this work cannot do it in the way in which the intellectual Liberal of the nineteenth century used to work. He cannot regard himself as a spectator, free to 'look on' at life—free from men and society, indifferent to, and detached from material conditions, and only admitting his personal passions or his own observations. The intellectual who wants to understand the present world must regard himself on the level of other men, with them subject to the same laws, to the same influences, to the same despair, destined for the same death. And it is for them, but also for himself, that he ought to become aware, that he ought to be aroused from this nightmare in which technics has plunged the world. He ought to consider himself in this world, whose inner structure he perceives as involved in this civilization, moved by it, dependent on it, but also, perhaps, capable of altering it.

He must commit himself to this enterprise, and must try to see, in a concrete way, what the world is, and see himself in it, in a concrete way. This is not the hour for Utopias, nor for political realism: it is the hour 'for becoming aware,' which claims the life of everyone, for indeed, everyone who thus commits himself accepts the fact that his whole life is 'committed.' He enters into a genuine drama, not a figurative one. This simply means that one cannot be a Communist intellectual and put aside a nice little capital sum, like the kind of scholar one knows so well, or it means that one cannot be an anarchist writer and have contracts with respectable publishers, that one cannot be a proletarian poet and travel first-class. On the intellectual level, it is the same offence as it is for a Christian to be a banker; on the economic level, it is the failure to commit one's life, it is the failure to be aware of the world, it is the 'good conscience' which comes from the illusions of the kingdom of Satan.

Once more, in whose name are we to do and say such things? Thanks to what can we achieve this upheaval which seems impossible? At bottom, what this 'awareness' means, is the rediscovery in every sphere of life of the reality which all the world is seeking. And what shall we do by ourselves in this argument? How are we to come to know this spiritual reality which conditions material reality? (We see it, indeed, in experience, but we cannot go any further.)

In short, to achieve this awareness as a whole is only possible under the illumination of the Holy Spirit. Here we are pulled up sharply—we can go no further. We can see what is necessary, and many people have been able, until now, to agree about this, but we have not found either the means or the reason, that is, the motive force to achieve it. And how people search for it, and how they go round and round in circles! For thousands of years man has been turning the same water-wheel above an empty well. Whatever work is undertaken by man does not reveal its meaning or its value save in Jesus Christ and through the Holy Spirit. Appearances change nothing, but we cannot develop this statement here any further.

We ought at least, however, to state clearly the extreme dilemma in which we find ourselves. In reality all systems of interpretation, of understanding of our civilization, are included in it (including dialectical materialism, which is an integral part of this world which may be described as 'bourgeois,' and including surrealism, which is an obvious element of this world which may be described as 'traditional').

Nothing which this world suggests is any use for this effort to 'become aware.' For this we need a truth which illuminates the intelligence of man with a much greater light. We also need an authority which inevitably commits man in the act of comprehension. We need a power which reveals to man the authenticity of the setting in which he is placed. All this cannot come from man. For centuries man has been able to delude himself by thinking that he is placed in a world which he considers 'normal'; this does not mean 'good' but a world 'suitable for human beings.' Nowadays such illusions are no longer possible, save for the insane. We are now confronted by an unavoidable choice, by the structure of this world itself, and the intellectual can no longer give good reasons for remaining simply what he is. In other words, to-day neither intellectual effort nor activity can possibly bring us to this awareness of the world in which we live. Now it is necessary to have an exterior intervention because our civilization is absolutely totalitarian, and we cannot extricate ourselves from it. But there is no longer any exterior force in the world. Our society absorbs all forms of intelligence. Thus, because our civilization is more than human, we must perceive that it is not made by 'flesh and blood' but by the 'principalities . . . and . . . powers . . . the world-rulers of this darkness . . .'[1] But nothing in our intellectual training prepares us either to see or to understand this. Our intellectual methods are purely materialistic, and entirely inadequate for such profound awareness to become possible. It is, indeed, true that it is only the intervention of the Holy Spirit which can transform our intelligence, in such a way that it will not be swallowed up by our systems, and that it will be sufficiently penetrating. To-day no other possibility exists. Until now the normal intelligence of man was enough, but in our present civilization all that it can produce is the 'brave new world' of Aldous Huxley.

It is absolutely essential that Christian intellectuals

[1] Eph. 6.12.

should understand the decisive character of our epoch, and that if we were to renounce this effort to become aware of it, an effort which demands the whole of our personality, we would be traitors to God, and the vocation which He has given us, but we would also be traitors to the world in which we live, in spite of all the good will that we may bring to the effort to solve social or economic problems, in spite of devotion to various good causes, in spite of our zeal for the progress of science, and so on. If we only do this, we shall merely be blind people leading other blind people to death.

This effort of 'awareness,' the one necessary act for the Christian intellectual of the present day, but an act which has to be continually renewed, implies, when one looks at it in its concrete reality, three consequences, and they are consequences which permit us precisely to say that this effort to achieve awareness is the solution of our present problems on the intellectual plane. (But we have seen that this awareness goes further than the intellectual plane; it issues from the Holy Spirit, to end in the wholehearted 'committal' of our lives to God.) These consequences also permit us to estimate whether our 'awareness' is genuine; finally, they are consequences which show that this 'awareness' is a specifically Christian act. These consequences may be summed up as follows: to rediscover the meaning of our neighbour, to rediscover the meaning of 'the Event,' to rediscover the limits of the Holy. These consequences will be briefly outlined in the following paragraphs, but without pretending to study them philosophically.

Decidedly, to-day communication has been broken because the intellectual is no longer 'neighbour' to anyone. He is no longer understood by other men because he no longer has anything in common with them. Whatever may be his concern for man, whatever may be his intellectual pre-occupations, other men are only strangers, separated from him. It is very evident that it is the duty of every Christian to become 'neighbour' to someone, but for the intellectual this is still more urgent, because this is an operation which justifies his very presence—because it ought to be conscious—because he must now create something new. Our world, by the very fact of its existence, breaks personal relations; men have, however, also undertaken to do this consciously and scientifically: the Nazis and the Communists by concentrating the whole idea of evil in 'the enemy.' The man by whom one is confronted is no longer merely 'the enemy,' he is the expression of evil itself: on the one hand 'the Jew,' the 'Communist,' the 'plutocrat.' On the other, the 'bourgeois,' the 'saboteur,' the 'Trotskyist' incarnates all evil upon earth, and in consequence we ought to kill him without pity, for he is no longer a human being, he is a symbol.

Similarly, in the opposite sense, the most important thing that we can do socially is to rediscover our neighbour. Christianity achieves this of itself, it is a product of faith. The man who confronts us is no longer merely one like ourselves, but 'the brother for whom Christ died.' Now this attitude, which ought to be that of every Christian, springing directly out of his faith, can be consciously determined and deliberately directed by the Christian intellectual. It is not a simple matter to become 'neighbour' to someone. There is, of

course, the study of what this means which can be
undertaken theologically, and we can study the theological basis of this relationship. This has already been
done, and in consequence I do not wish to dwell on
this point. But it is not a simple thing in our civilization, which, as I have already said, tends to the rupture
of personal relations, that is to say, tends to prevent this
relationship. By his effort to achieve awareness, the
intellectual rediscovers a sphere in which he can be in
relation with other men: the point of contact with
reality. But the characteristic work to-day of the
Christian intellectual is to discover a new language, a
language which helps men to understand one another,
in spite of publicity, a language which permits men to
abandon their despairing solitude, and avoids both
rational sterility and subjective emotionalism. The
search for a new language which will give a purer
meaning to the words of the tribe, with all that this
means of submission to the real (our language is totally
dissociated from the real) and an adaptation to different
mental structures, a language which should be a
living expression of the words of St. Paul, 'all things
to all men.'

For the Christian intellectual this problem of language is the key-problem to contact with other men.
Other people, too, have felt this need. Other people
have sought for this language, but they have only
ended up in a more hopeless solitude, like that of the
Surrealists.

It is normal that men should be separate and
strangers, but the Holy Spirit creates communication
between them, and enables them to break through this
separation. The Holy Spirit alone can do this, the Holy
Spirit alone can establish this link with one's neighbour.

The Holy Spirit alone can open our eyes and ears, not only to revealed truth, but to the humble love of men. But man must work patiently at that which the Holy Spirit uses. If man flees into the desert, if he hides himself away, alone, in a hermit life, there will be no neighbours, and then what can the Holy Spirit do? If man, in our civilization, does not recreate a possible language, there is no support for the action of the Holy Spirit, there are no human means which God always demands from men when He wishes to manifest his power. The Holy Spirit alone can give meaning, truth, and effectiveness to this language, but men must have sought for it. Christians no longer seek it because they believe that neighbourly relations are quite simple, that the situation is the same as it used to be, that that which succeeded a thousand years ago will succeed to-day. Now at different times, in the course of Christian history, Christians have rediscovered a language. To-day they do not seem to mind about this—it is the non-Christians who seek it, but up till now the Holy Spirit has not honoured this quest.

It is urgent that Christian intellectuals should rediscover the meaning of their vocation along this line. Everything has to be done, but it is the only way of rediscovering a method of comprehension beyond all classes, formulas, and political divisions. It is the only way of breaking through the sociological trends which separate us, and rediscovering genuine personal relationships in love. It is to-day the only way in which we can live in love without the fatal sentimentalism with which liberalism, both intellectual and theological, had infected the idea of our 'neighbour.' If we do not invent this language all our preaching of love cannot be understood by men.

A second consequence of this effort to achieve awareness shows us a second task, a second duty for the
Christian intellectual. The man who believes in tri-
fling incidents, and interprets them by the myth, no
longer believes in 'the event,' that is to say, in the
intervention of one fact in the course of life, of history,
of development, which brings with it a certain modification, which includes within itself the meaning of all the
development of the past, and significance for the future.
The 'event' is the opposite of incidental facts, because
it is charged with experience, and grips man as a whole.
The 'event' is also the opposite of the modern 'myth,'
because it bears its meaning within itself, because the
adhesion which it requires is personal, and leads man
to a personal decision.

But to believe in 'the event' is to have a certain conception of history which the event is able to produce
within it. Now, actually, not only the material conditions which we have discussed tend to make us reject
the 'event,' but also the dominating conceptions, both
of history and of the life of the individual, tend to
deny 'the event.' Several times I have said that modern
man lives in a dream, and that when he is struggling
for some purely material end he does not meet material
reality but abstractions; this statement could be otherwise expressed: none of the facts which take place in
the world, or in his personal life, have any real independent meaning for the individual; they do not lead him
to an experience, and a decision, but, on the contrary,
they always seem to be the product of collective power,
of a sociological action. So, there is no 'event,' no
faith is possible. There is only the artificial myth. It is
this attitude to life which explains the modern success of
certain political systems, and, at the same time, the

lack of interest in the Christian Faith. It is the consequence, in the religious sphere, of the impossibility of
grasping the reality of the actual world.

Further, if there is no event, there cannot be any
personal and voluntary action on the part of man in
history and on his life. All that is left is passive acceptance of authority in every sphere of life. Now the
problem is twofold. We need to know, objectively,
whether there is the possibility of the event in history,
and also if there is an event in the life of man from the
individual point of view.

The recognition of 'the event' in our world is a consequence of our awareness, and this work of the Christian
intellectual seems absolutely necessary, in order to give
a new meaning to the life of our fellow-men at the
present day. But to rediscover the 'event,' its meaning
and its significance to-day, is not an arbitrary piece of
work nor is it something which can be constructed from
the purely intellectual point of view. We are not here
dealing with a philosophy of 'the event' which would be
based only upon human reason, for nothing could
prove that 'the event' actually exists. If Christians
have a special mission here, it is due to the fact that
they are witnesses to an event on which all other events
are based, an event which took place in history, and an
event which is produced in the life of men, an event
which sums up and guarantees all other events, personal
or historical, and renders history and life absolutely
irreversible. This event is the intervention of God in the
course of human history, it is Jesus Christ. Here there
is no question of reducing this event to a philosophical
formula. This is the great danger which dogs our steps,
for this work would reduce our certainty to nothing.

What matters is not that 'eternity has intervened in

time,' or that 'an abstract God has intervened for man.'
When we speak aright about 'the Event' we say that it
is in the living man, Jesus, that the living God has
incarnated Himself. From this standpoint, and from
this alone, it is possible for the intellectual to rediscover
this sphere, indispensable for thought and for life,
which is the actual event. From this point of view, and
from it alone, we can call men to experience personally
and to rediscover the meaning of life, and of the relation
which God creates between Jesus Christ and life, not
only the life which is called 'Eternal,' but the life of
every day. 'Unto them that are without, all things
are done in parables . . . and how shall ye know *all*
the parables?'[1] Thus we are charged to understand
all these parables which express the action of Jesus
Christ, in history and in the life of man; and it is this
comprehension alone that can give them meaning. It
is only in Jesus Christ that we have any possibility of
understanding this wild adventure on which we have
started, for in the midst of these shadows He is there, the
Person, the Event, in the midst of these whirlwinds of
facts, the Author and the Finisher of our faith. Instead
of losing ourselves in idle speculation, or in futile
political and social agitation, as the world does, here is
the great genuine task of Christian intellectuals: by
means of this event to give once more direction to the
world in the spheres of politics, social conditions, and
many others, and, in this event, to help them to find a
hope which is no illusion.

There is now one final consequence of this effort to
achieve awareness which will show us how urgent is the

[1] Mark 4.11–13.

work of the intellectual for the Church and for the world—how no one else can do this work; how, finally, at the present time, Christians alone have the actual possibility of responding to these needs, the possibility which has been granted them (it has not always been so, and from the point of view of the absolute, it is not the only possible solution).

We have seen how the intelligence has become enslaved to the means of expression at its disposal. The problem for the liberation of the intelligence is to restore intellectual techniques. Now we have seen that to the extent to which the intelligence has only one means of expression, namely, the most effective, it cannot absolutely be free from it and act in a different way in the world; and, finally, it is not in artificially creating another means of expression that we shall achieve this. We have already seen why this is so.

In reality, the solution of this problem lies, strange as it may seem, in the discovery of the border-line between the profane and the sacred (not the religious or the Christian, but the 'sacred' or the 'holy' in the sense in which—more or less—this phrase is used by Otto). But this does not consist in an artificial creation of two spheres, in carving out a sphere by means of human reason; it is the recognition by the intelligence that two spheres exist. It is the gradual discovery of the frontier which exists in the facts between the two spheres. It is the fact that intellectual action, with its methods of modern investigation, has the right to go to the very border of the 'Holy,' but no further.

Now, in concrete terms, we know that it is possible to invade the Sacred. Man can suppress it, destroy it, and then deny it. He can violate, by mechanical means, what is beyond his reach, and this is why we are perishing in the application of the intelligence to man and to the social sphere. We have upset the balance of the world, and of man, by our powerful techniques. This comes out in detail as well as in the main framework of life. We have destroyed one of the elements of equilibrium in our world by applying, without discrimination, our intellectual instruments to all spheres of life. To rediscover the limits of the Holy, to go as far as we can in the use in the intellect, but to stop willingly when we are in danger of invading the sphere of the Holy, this is one of the main functions of the intellectual search. We must not hide from ourselves that this gives a different orientation to research, and this may seem to be a limitation: this suggests that one possesses criteria of judgment which are outside and above the intelligence; that the latter is not free to do all that is possible to it; it can do everything, but it ought not to wish to do everything it can; what we need to rediscover is intellectual self-control. This will bring with it the refusal of certain means, the refusal of certain methods of intervention, for the doctor, the physicist, the biologist, but also for the jurist, the economist, and the man who studies agriculture from the scientific point of view. Further, it is a limitation in that the intelligence is led to admit that such a sphere ought to remain beyond its reach, or more or less beyond the sphere of its technical methods. But it is the only way open to us at the present time to give back to the intelligence its authentic power, and to give technics its place in the real world. For the intelligence, in rediscovering this frontier, also finds in so doing the reality of the world and the possibility of renewed action. For it rediscovers the inner structure of the world. Under an apparent diminution of its effectiveness, the intelligence really attains its own equilibrium; it becomes effective in another way. It sees that action is possible through this spiritual structure, action upon the world. Thus vast possibilities arise which our intellectual method has caused to disappear. I do not mean that we are to monopolize the Holy, nor to try to influence it intellectually, but the intelligence can, in ways other than those of technics, find the means of influencing the material world by the intermediary means of the Holy. This is actually the only fact which can save our intellectual system from the disaster which threatens it. Further, I have not many illusions about the possibilities of a material renunciation for the sake of the spiritual.

Now, actually, Christianity alone enables us to find the dividing line between the profane and the sacred. All that sociologists or psychologists can tell us is limited, limited to man; and considered also from the angle of an 'object of science,' which is no use at all. What the other religions are able to show is the Holy alone, and they are now out of date, for at the present time the situation in this sphere is so complex, and so desperate, that here again only an intervention of the Holy Spirit can give to the intelligence of man sufficient clarity, and sufficient self-control, to do this work. Doubtless, in the Bible there is a great deal of teaching about this twofold sphere. Constantly we find this sphere of the sacred, in man and in nature, not so much as something religious and in connexion with salvation, but as something which constitutes the order of the world willed by God for its preservation. The sacred is no longer close to God, it is part of this world, but there is an essential part which is found outside our sacrilegious hands, because God has arranged it thus. Only, it is not sufficient to know this objectively, to find it in the Scriptures, for this never shows us the actual application, nor does it indicate to us a border-line for our own day. On the other hand, this does not assure us of the obedience of the intelligence to-day, which in its pride and madness, believes it can do anything, and refuses all wisdom. This can only come from the admission of a superior authority which is imposed from outside on the mind of man, and gives him a rule, while at the same time it restores to him his genuine function.

To sum up, in the intellectual sphere, in connexion with political and social spheres, we need a complete revision of all our positions, a new beginning, and this reconstruction cannot be the work of one man alone, it cannot be exclusively the work of man.

This work is necessary, not only for the intellectual, but for all men, for if Christians do not do this work, they cannot have any hope for all that concerns their attitude in the social or political world, all that they will be able to do there will be puerile, useless, and out-of-date at the present day. It is disastrous to see Christians embarking in all the social and political boats of this world, entirely unaware of all the preliminary questions which they alone could examine.

Christian intellectuals must go forward to this great process of questioning, for the world, which is wandering about in a labyrinth made by its own hands; and for the Church, which should now at last break through all its ready-made intellectual categories, and for the other members of the Church who ought to receive genuine teaching on the life of faith.

The work of Christian intellectuals is not done in the abstract, it is effective participation in the preservation of the world, and in the building up of the Church. This is why we cannot act here simply in a free way; this is not an intellectual gymnastic to which we are called; it is, above all, in prayer and meditation that intellectuals will rediscover the sources of an intelligent life rooted in the concrete.

V

PROLOGUE AND
CONCLUSION

IN the preceding pages we have only been able to give
some very summary and fragmentary suggestions.
Our aim was not to give ready-made solutions, but only
to open the way for a work of the renewed Church.
That is why these pages, which are a conclusion to this
study, are also a prologue to more extended study which
would examine the problem of our present civilization
from every aspect, including its concrete effects on the
Church and on Christians everywhere. If only my
fellow-Christians are stirred by the present study to feel
the urgency and the depth of these questions, the time
spent in writing this book will not have been lost, either
for me or for them.

I am aware that all that I have written may seem
rather intellectual, and even abstract. I was very
anxious, however, not to toy with philosophical speculation, nor to deal with these world problems in a
bookish or literary way. But, after all, this world of
ours *is* very complicated: far more so than the preceding epochs. If we are to understand it in any comprehensive way, we need a vast amount of knowledge.
All that I have written practically amounts to a kind of

synthesis of a large *number of facts*. In my description of
the contemporary scene, behind each bare statement
lies an experience; and I could support each statement
with concrete examples. To do this, however, would
require more leisure than my present circumstances
permit, for the time is short. All that I have written is
based on precise and well-known facts. But we usually
pass through these facts like shadows in a kingdom of
shadows. Day after day the wind blows away the
pages of our calendars, our newspapers, and our political
régimes, and we glide along the stream of time without
any spiritual framework, without a memory, without
a judgment, carried about by 'all winds of doctrine'
on the current of history, which is always slipping into
a perpetual past. Now we ought to react vigorously
against this slackness—this tendency to drift. If we are
to *live* in this world we need to know it far more profoundly; we need to rediscover the meaning of events,
and the spiritual frame-work which our contemporaries
have lost. This will be a difficult enterprise, for it is
new and humble. But 'all things are ours,' that is, for
us, as Christians, and we *are* able to undertake this new
work.

Let us go back to the simplest position. One primary
statement of fact, which stands out clearly when we
reflect upon our Church life, and our Christian action,
is the fundamental weakness of our evangelization.
The countries which are supposed to possess a Christian
civilization are rapidly becoming secularized, and people
listen to the Church less and less. Meanwhile missions
in Africa and Asia are making slow progress; the peoples
of these countries are already drifting into decadence,

before they have known the stimulus of Christianity. The world as a whole no longer listens to the Gospel. The Word of God no longer penetrates into the reality of human life. Men seek other solutions, listen to other promises, to other gospels. Every Christian worth his salt is seriously disturbed by this situation. We could easily carry this diagnosis of our situation further, but what matters is this: why are we in this condition and what can we do about it?

We are not the first people to ask these questions; many others have done so already. All kinds of answers have been given, all of which seem to me to be superficial. For, in my view, to-day we are called to nothing less than the recognition of the fact that we need above all to understand the strategy the Devil is using to neutralize the Gospel. Unless we see this clearly, we understand nothing. Thus we ought to have a very exact knowledge of the full reality of the situation before we can hope to win any response. The Gospel no longer penetrates. We seem to be confronted by a blank wall. Now if we want to go further: either, we must find a door, or, we must break down the wall! But first of all we must investigate this wall, in order to find out whether there *is* a door: thus we need to explore this world in which we are now living. If there *is* no door (as seems to me to be the case) then we must find (or create) the instruments we need in order to make a breach in it. All the preceding chapters of this book have really been a search for these instruments, by means of which we may penetrate through this thick wall, against which at present the Gospel is battering in vain.

I know very well that people will say to me, 'But what's the good of all this labour? Isn't simple preaching enough?' In reality this so-called confidence in the 'efficacy of the Word of God' betrays a lack of charity towards men, and an indifference to their actual situation; to some extent it is a 'spirituality' which is not in accordance with the mind of Christ. The Bible always shows us God laying hold of man in his practical situation, in the setting of his life, enabling him to act with the means of his own time, in the midst of the problems of his own day. But to want to copy the methods of Irenaeus or of Calvin means that we are both mistaken and unfaithful. If we think of the problems of the contemporary world in the terms in which St. Augustine or Luther described the problems of their own time we are mistaken and ineffective. Now, our own day presents very complicated problems; our organization is more complex than that of past centuries, and the same is true of the questions which challenge the Christian faith and conscience. Every day man seems less capable of dominating his own time, but this is not the moment to copy John the Baptist and to say: 'Let's preach in the desert! The wall may be there, but all *we* have to do is to preach! God will see to it that our message is heard!'

We cannot use this great word of St. Paul, 'I planted . . . but God gave the increase'[1]—we cannot give everything into the hands of God (believing that God will open the eyes, ears, and hearts of men), until we have wrestled with God till the break of day, like Jacob; that is, until we have struggled to the utmost limits of our strength, and have known the despair of defeat. If we do not do this, our so-called 'confidence' in God, and our 'orthodoxy' are nothing less than hypocrisy, cowardice, and laziness. All that I have

---

[1] 1 Cor. 3.6–7.

already written will be useless unless it is understood as a call to arms, showing what enemy we have to confront, what warfare we have to wage, what weapons we have to use. Then, in the heart of this conflict, the Word can be proclaimed, but nowhere else. When we have really understood the actual plight of our contemporaries, when we have heard their cry of anguish, and when we have understood why they won't have anything to do with our 'disembodied' Gospel, when we have shared their sufferings, both physical and spiritual, in their despair and their desolation, when we have become one with the people of our own nation and of the universal Church, as Moses and Jeremiah were one with their own people, as Jesus identified Himself with the wandering crowds, 'sheep without a shepherd,' *then* we shall be able to proclaim the Word of God—but not till then!

To proclaim the word of God to men in the abstract, to people who are in a situation which prevents them from understanding it, means that we are tempting God. Let us meditate once more on that incisive saying of our Lord: 'Give not that which is holy unto the dogs, neither cast your pearls before the swine, lest haply they trample them under their feet, and turn and rend you.'[1] This is a striking description of the relation between the Church and the world at the present time. The Church, which has received the 'pearls' of the Gospel, throws them with pious indifference as food to the 'swine,' who are human beings (and this includes ourselves, 'good Christians') embedded in the clay of this world, which is so exclusively materialistic, submerged by economic and political problems, by their personal fears and their financial worries, by their

[1] Matt. 7.6.

anxieties and their daily troubles, absolutely dominated by the spirit of the present age. And these people turn against the Church, saying: 'We find no nourishment in your pearls, no satisfaction in their beauty. What are we to do with them? They are no good to us in our present situation!' (And this is true!) And they attack the Church which has only given them fair words and illusions—they want to tear it down. These people are wrong, for the Word of God is always valid, and if they do not get anything from it to-day, it is because they are in a false position: it is not the Word which needs to be changed, and to bring them something, it is their own position which needs to be changed. But they are right in their feeling about the Church, because it is the Church which ought to initiate this changed situation, in order that the Word of God may be heard in human life as a whole. And the Church has no right to confine itself to 'casting pearls before swine.' First of all, the Church should do some preparatory work, in order that 'the swine' may be able to receive 'the pearls.' It is not for the Church to separate human beings into two categories—first of all the 'swine' (Communists, non-'conformists,' people who have 'mistaken ideas,' working-men, and so on) to whom we cannot proclaim the Gospel; and, secondly, those who are not 'swine,' those dull good 'sheep,' which our world creates in such numbers!

What the Church ought to do is to try to place all men in an economic, intellectual, yes, and also in a psychological and physical situation, which is such that they can actually *hear* this Gospel—that they can be sufficiently responsible to say 'yes' or 'no,' that they can be sufficiently alive for these words to have some meaning for them. The secret of their choice belongs to God, but they should be able to make a decision; it is 'up to the Church' to see to it that they are not placed in such conditions that they cannot react otherwise than as 'swine,' to whom 'pearls' have been thrown. 'Cast not your pearls before swine'—but men must cease to be 'swine,' and this is not the work of Grace, it is a human work, which man is quite able to achieve, though it is terribly difficult to do; Christians in particular are called to this work, because it is possible for them to see the true situation of man better than other people, and because, better than others, they can see where all this ought to lead, and what is its aim.

We need a revolution, in a world in which it has become impossible; a revolution which attacks the bases of a civilization whose efforts tend solely towards transforming men into 'swine'—all men—who by this very fact can no longer receive the divine 'pearls.' We need a rediscovery of the meaning of human activity, of the relation between means and ends, of their true place in a world which is given up to the love of power, to disorder, to the pride based on a sense of limitless power over the external world.

We need a new form of communication between human beings, in order that the relations between them, distorted by their conditions of life, by class feeling, by prejudice, may, by a renewal of their intelligence, be recreated upon a personal and living plane.

This is where we ought to start, in order to act in the world, and to work to transform the material conditions of the world. Apart from this, without these 'lines of force,' Christians can only make sporadic efforts, without co-ordination, without a profound judgment, and often in the wrong direction, in spite of any amount of goodwill. In so doing, we need to avoid two errors: the first error consists in adopting, purely and simply, one of the attitudes of the world, that which seems to be most in harmony with the Christian ideal, and then, becoming Communist, Liberal, Pacifist, Personalist, and so on, according to one's taste and sentiment, which we then justify by appealing to some Christian truth. But to do this, under the pretext of being 'in the world,' actually means belonging to the world. Christians who do this are no longer acting as 'leaven' in the world—they have capitulated to it. They are no longer carrying on a dialogue with the world; they are simply agreeing with the world, walking in the same way, adopting its method, and, in spite of appearances, they are simply fostering the Devil's work in the world. On the other hand, it would also be a mistake simply to search the Scriptures for the order of God for this world, and then to present it objectively, holding up the picture before the world, and being quite satisfied with this ideological effort, expecting the world, by some mysterious process of imitation, obediently to follow what is suggested, and to accept this divine order. In reality, this attitude means renouncing action in the world, in spite of concrete declarations which might be made as a result of these studies, possibly even, in spite of definite proposals for reform. Here, again, Christians are not acting as 'leaven' in the world, they are simply giving advice and enunciating doctrine.

In fact, in both instances, what is lacking is the intermediate position: this perpetual 'missing link,' which arrests our Christian action. I believe that we *can* discover it, in conclusions which we draw from the Lordship of Jesus Christ, both present and eschatological. In the light of this fact we have tried to show what it means to be 'Christians in the modern world,' but this is only one aspect, on which we have dwelt because it seemed to us that it is the one which is least recognized and most urgent.

In order that Christianity to-day may have a point of contact with the world, it is less important to have theories about economic and political questions, or even to take up a definite political and economic position, than it is to create a new style of life. It is evident that the first thing to do is to be faithful to revelation, but this fidelity can only become a reality in daily life through the creation of this new way of life: this is the 'missing link.' There used to be a 'style of life' peculiar to the Middle Ages. In the sixteenth century, there was a 'style of life' carried on by Reformed Church Christians, and it is extremely interesting to note where it was opposed to the 'style of life' of the Renaissance. There is the bourgeois 'style of life,' which has no spiritual quality at all; there is the Communist 'style of life'; there is no longer a Christian 'style of life.' To speak quite frankly, without beating about the bush, a doctrine only has power (apart from that which God gives it) to the extent in which it creates a style of life, to the extent in which it is adopted, believed, and accepted by men who have a style of life which is in harmony with it. Marxist thought has only made such strides because it saw clearly the true situation of the people by whom it was confronted, and because it was strongly supported by a style of life imposed on men by economic and social conditions. The extreme weakness of Liberalism or of Socialism is due to the fact that it is no longer connected with any 'style of life.' The *bourgeoisie* is increasingly losing its own style, and all that it retains is a worn-out tradition, out of touch with reality. The 'working-class *élite*,' has never had its own distinctive 'style of life'; it has only had a pale imitation of the *bourgeoisie*. In point of fact, the only people to-day who have a 'style of life' are the proletarian 'masses'; but the element that seems new is this: that instead of springing from a choice, from a creation—as at the time of the Renaissance—the latter is imposed by its kind of life, by its work, by its social position. In spite of its enforced character, we do see here a style of life, which is original (that is to say, distinct from others), the creator of a mental structure and of a new ethic, forming an organic solidarity between those who adopt it; and, finally, because it manifests a profound agreement between the individual and the social group of which it forms a part.

When we seek to discover effective action for the Church, owing to the necessity for its intervention in the world, it seems as though its first objective should be the creation of a style of life. For if we consider the life of Christians in our churches, we see certainly that they make good sons, fathers, husbands, employers, and workmen—'good, like good bread,' said Aragon—they have many individual virtues, but they have no style of life, or rather, they have exactly that which has been imposed upon them by their sociological conditions: that is to say, by their social class, their nation, their environment, and so on. It is not their *spiritual* condition which affects their style of life: it is their political or economic condition, and from this point of view, they are an overwhelming demonstration of the truth, temporary and temporal, of Marxism. Now at the present time, many Christians are fully aware that this is an intolerable situation, and that if it is allowed to go on, it will prepare the way for the total collapse of the Churches of the West. This problem of the style of life is absolutely central; for it is at this point that the question of the integration of Christianity into the world, or at least of its creative power, will be most fiercely tested.

This will be the 'turn-table' on which all the ways which have been gradually opened up by the patient efforts of the Church will end. This includes the Ecumenical Movement, for the Universal Church must manifest itself as such in the life of Christians, whatever their position may be, or their links with other sociological groups. It also includes the life of professional associations, for the effort to integrate one's faith in one's profession ends in creating a new style of life. It also includes the search for a Christian culture, or of a method of evangelizing the world-wide proletariat, which is true and concrete, as well as the discovery of a new life within the parishes, and in the beliefs of the Church.

The creation of such a style of life is a work which is both collective and individual. It is a fact for each Christian, who really tries to express his faith in the concrete forms of his life. It is also the task of Christians as a corporate body, where all these efforts, sometimes differing widely, sometimes even contradictory, are recorded. It does not matter whether all these efforts are in logical agreement. The formation of a style of life could not be the result of a doctrine, firmly and clearly established, which it would then be sufficient to put into practice. On the contrary it is the fact of living in faith; consequently it cannot satisfy us on the administrative or intellectual plane. But it is here that

doctrine finds its human basis, and its power for action.
On the other hand, it is very evident that ecclesiastical
bodies, and 'prophets,' too, can lead the 'flock' of the
Church in a certain sense, by the formation of this
style of life—can evoke new enquiries, and can support
those who are risking something in this adventure of the
spirit.

Now, as its name indicates, the whole of life is concerned in this search. It includes the way we think
about present political questions, as well as our way of
practising hospitality. It also affects the way we dress
and the food we eat (our austere *bourgeois* friends ought
to understand that the problems of taste, fashion,
cooking, are important, if we are to form a style of life:
but it is not sufficient to be simply 'in the fashion'—
it is, indeed, the opposite—or to 'choose the best
(commercial) quality,' which has nothing to do with
it!) as well as the way in which we manage our financial
affairs. It includes being faithful to one's wife as well
as being accessible to one's neighbour. It includes the
position one ought to take on current social and political
questions, as well as the decisions which relate to the
personal employment of our time.

I could multiply these examples, which are mere
suggestions, to show that absolutely everything, the
smallest details which we regard as indifferent, ought to
be questioned, placed in the light of faith, examined
from the point of view of the glory of God. It is on this
condition that, in the Church, we might possibly
discover a new style of Christian life, voluntary and
true. I will refrain from giving a positive content to
these suggestions; and I will not try to describe this
'style of life.' First of all, because it would not correspond to anything, since at present there is no reality

in this sphere. At the moment such a description would be a purely intellectual theory. For the moment, it is sufficient to suggest to Christian people that such a change is necessary. Increasingly, we ought to try to form such an idea, through Bible study, and different ways of learning to understand the world in which we are living. Further, because such a description would eventually be too easy a spring-board for Christians who might try to turn it into a new law, we must go on repeating that if this style of life is not made by Christians it will not have any meaning. Finally, because, as I suggested above, the actual attempts are varied and unco-ordinated, and it will not do to force them into a synthesis without respect for the truths they represent.

There is, however, one very important truth which needs to be stressed: namely, that such research is necessarily a corporate act. It is impossible for an isolated Christian to follow this path. I believe, in fact, that one of the essential conditions for its realization is the substitution of a true solidarity among Christians (a solidarity—voluntarily created by obedience to the will of God) for the sociological solidarity, purely mechanical in character, which is being dinned into our ears, and which people want to make the basis of the new world. In order to undertake this search for a new 'style of life,' every Christian ought to feel and to know that he is supported by others, not only for spiritual and ideological reasons—because, for instance, of the difficulty of the problems that our world sets for man—but also for purely material reasons: for example, for a workman, for a minor employee, the question of a choice in his way of living or in his trade, is immediately expressed in terms of money. So long as the solidarity between Christians is not expressed in mutual help, which will permit everyone to find a balanced life, to discover a style of life which truly expresses his faith (and not in order to avoid starving), it will only be a matter of words. This alone shows us this search may lead us into paths which are very disagreeable to our cherished habits. In actual fact, it will be very disagreeable, but it is at this price that the good news of salvation in Christ will be something different from a human word among other human words.

Further it will evidently be necessary to engage in a work which aims at rebuilding parish life, at discovering Christian community, so that people may learn afresh what the fruit of the Spirit is (a very different thing from human 'virtues'). We shall need to rediscover the concrete application of self-control, liberty, unity, and so on. All this is essential for the life of the Church, and the function of Christianity in the world. And all this ought to be directed towards the preaching and the proclamation of the Gospel. This is another aspect of this whole effort to live as Christians in the world, an aspect which is far better known, if not in its content, at least in its necessity; that is why we do not need to outline it further here. Before I conclude, however, there is one more step to take.

We have constantly tried to show how the action of God through Christians could solve the problem of the world; that Christians are in such a situation (placed by God in this situation) that they can respond. And yet they ought not to take themselves too seriously, for the danger which menaces the Church in this necessary struggle is that of becoming merely a sociological movement—that is, if the Church takes herself too seriously, and tries to bear the weight of the whole effort alone. Were this to happen, the Church would then only be another secular movement: it would be nationalist if nationalism were strong; it would be 'Bergsonian' if the world offered it this way of escape from rationalism! It would become authoritarian if the general political tendency were moving that way! It would support the idea of 'community' when it was in fashion; and it would be in favour of 'colonization' when the world was in favour of it—only to abandon all these views the moment that they had ceased to be fashionable! At another time the Church would be Socialist or Communist, because there seemed to be an apparent victory of the Left in Europe! But a Church that behaves like this, is a Church which has ceased to be a 'leaven' in the life of the world. Of course, in each case that I have mentioned, there are always theological arguments to justify such action, for nations are ruled by God and 'colonization helps the proclamation of the Gospel,' or 'social justice is an authentic expression of the justice of God.' But all these phrases are simply efforts to justify ourselves, in spite of the theological truth which they contain. Now when the Church is in this position, it is no longer the salt of the earth, or the light of the world. It is no more than one of the forms in which the will of the world is expressed, and actually it is helping the world to realize its own ends. It no longer represents the power of the action of God in the world.

Of course, this does not mean that the Church must cut itself off completely from these movements in the

world. First of all because the Church is composed of
people who are living in their own time, and it cannot
ignore these efforts, which do represent an aspect of
truth. The Church is necessarily deeply involved in all
this movement, because it is still on earth. But the
Church should be aware of the position. For instance,
if it succumbs to the temptation of Socialism, it should
be aware that this does not come from God, but from
the world, and that it is a compromise, though doubtless
an inevitable one; it should realize that though this
might have a certain value, this value has neither been
chosen nor created by the Church, and that its justifica-
tion carries little weight. It ought to know also, that
almost always these 'compromises' have turned out
badly for the Church, and *in consequence*, they have been
disastrous for the world.

Here are three instances of what I mean—it would be
easy to find others:

(*a*) The Church, subjected by its compromise with
the State under Constantine or Louis XIV.

(*b*) The Church disintegrated by its compromise
with Capitalism in the nineteenth century.

(*c*) The Church deprived of revealed truth by its
compromise with science at the same epoch.

Confronted by these compromises, the Church ought
not to justify itself, or to justify the world's solution, but
it ought to find its own way, given it by God, which it
alone can follow. It is only on this condition that the
Church will cease to be a sociological movement, and be
present in the world with the effectiveness given by the
Holy Spirit.

The enemies of the Church seek to turn it aside from
its own way, in order to make it follow their way; the
moment it yields it becomes the play-thing of the forces

of the world. It is given up to its adversaries. It can only have recourse to God in prayer, that He may teach it His way, which no one else can teach it. This means not only the way of eternal salvation, but the way which one follows in the land of the living, the way which is truly impossible to find unless God reveals it, truly impossible to follow with our human power alone. The problem is the same in the social and the individual sphere. From the human point of view this way of the Church in the world is foolish, Utopian, and ineffective, and we are seized with discouragement when we see what we really have to do in this real world. We might throw the whole thing up, were we not sure of seeing the goodness of the Lord in the land of the living: but we have seen this goodness, it has been manifested, and on this foundation we can go forward and confront the powers of this world, in spite of our impotence, for 'in all these things we are more than conquerors through Him that loved us. For I am persuaded that neither death nor life, nor angels nor principalities, nor things present, nor things to come, nor powers, nor height nor depth, nor any other creature, shall be able to separate us from the love of God which is in Christ Jesus our Lord.'[1]

[1] Rom. 8.37–39.